THE FUNCTION OF SACRIFICE IN CHRONICLES, EZRA, AND NEHEMIAH

THE FUNCTION OF SACRIFICE
IN CHRONICLES, EZRA,
AND NEHEMIAH

Mark Harold McEntire

MELLEN BIBLICAL PRESS

Library of Congress Cataloging-in-Publication Data

McEntire, Mark Harold, 1960-
    The function of sacrifice in Chronicles, Ezra, and Nehemiah / by
Mark Harold McEntire.
        p.   cm.
    Includes bibliographical references and index.
    ISBN 0-7734-2362-1
    1. Bible. O.T. Chronicles--Criticism, interpretation, etc.
2. Bible. O.T. Ezra--Criticism, interpretation, etc. 3. Bible.
O.T. Nehemiah--Criticism, interpretation, etc. 4. Sacrifice in the
Bible. I. Title.
BS1345.6.S24M34 1993
224--dc20   93-2688
                                                              CIP

A CIP catalog record for this book
is available from the British Library.

The Edwin Mellen Press   The Edwin Mellen Press
        Box 450   Box 67
  Lewiston, New York   Queenston, Ontario
    USA 14092   CANADA L0S 1L0

                Edwin Mellen Press, Ltd.
                Lampeter, Dyfed, Wales
                UNITED KINGDOM SA48 7DY

        Printed in the United States of America

To Mom and Dad

TABLE OF CONTENTS

Page

Chapter

Chapter 1

INTRODUCTION

The literary interpretations of Israel's history contained within the Hebrew Bible make apparent a people's need to understand and interpret its experience. While modern attempts at reconstructing a "true" history of Israel have made use of all the evidence contained in scripture, it has been the Deuteronomistic History which has attracted the most attention throughout the critical era. Meanwhile, the interpretation contained in the books of Chronicles, and continued in Ezra and Nehemiah, has suffered a lack of attention and considerable misuse. It is this literary deposit, however, which provides an interpretation of the experience of Israel from the very beginning through the Exile and on into the Restoration and construction of the second temple. While dating of these writings is tenuous, it is certain that Chronicles, Ezra, and Nehemiah emerged from the early post-Exilic era. Therefore, because of its content and date, it is this literature which offers the most vital interpretation of Israel's experience during and after the Exile.

The purpose of this study will be to examine Chronicles, Ezra, and Nehemiah, focusing on sacrifice as the key element, and to draw some conclusions about the community which is implied within the narrative. Reading the end of Chronicles and the beginning of Ezra, the only record of the Exile and Restoration in the Hebrew Bible, reveals a sudden concentration of sacrificial events bracketing the experience of exile. Though sacrifice is an important theme throughout the Bible, the number and character of the sacrificial events in the Chronistic material, especially in the remarkable section that runs from II Chronicles 29 - Ezra 6, is unprecedented. Focusing on these texts may lead to a new understanding of this interpretation of Israel's history. In addition it may be possible to discern the social function sacrifice served in the community portrayed in these texts. These ideas will be explored through the following steps: (1) Exegesis of the relevant texts in Chronicles, Ezra, and Nehemiah (2) development of the theology of sacrifice which emerges from the exegesis of the texts, (3) analysis of the social functions of sacrifice in the texts, in the light of modern theories, and (4) interpretive synthesis of all these factors.

Methodology

After an initial summary of the history of research in Chronicles, Ezra, and Nehemiah, the beginning point of this study will be a critical exegesis of the passages involving sacrificial events in II Chronicles and Ezra, and Nehemiah. The primary method will be redaction criticism, the purposes of which will be to demonstrate the centrality of sacrifice to these texts, and to provide the background for an understanding of the theology of sacrifice in the books involved. This process will include a comparison of the Chronicles and Ezra accounts to synoptic passages in Kings and I Esdras. An overall portrait of sacrifice in the books of Chronicles, Ezra, and Nehemiah will follow the individual examination of the selected passages.

In addition to the function sacrifice performs as an important element within this body of literature, it may also perform important social functions within the community described. The fourth chapter will present a comparison of some modern understandings of the social function of sacrifice with the events contained in Chronicles, Ezra, and Nehemiah which are discussed in chapters two and three. The preponderance of such events does lead to the question of why this material has such an intense interest in sacrifice. Hopefully, conclusions can be drawn as to the ways in which sacrifice operates as a social mechanism within the community implied in the text of Chronicles, Ezra, and Nehemiah. The resemblence of the community described in these narratives to the actual post-Exilic community is questionable. Any connections made between the social mechanisms of the two would be extremely tentative. No such connections are assumed in this work.

Summary of Research on Chronicles, Ezra, and Nehemiah

Research on Chronicles, Ezra, and Nehemiah has been dominated by four major areas of inquiry. The most vigorously pursued has been the question of unity of authorship. A second and related area involves proposed reconstructions of the textual history of these books. Third, there has been an increasing effort over the last few decades to outline the basic purposes or the theology of the author or authors. Finally, the chronological problems of the activity of Ezra and Nehemiah represent a mine field of confusion. Because all of these issues impinge in some way upon this study, some elements of each will be reviewed here. An attempt will also be made to judge the impact of each on this study.

Until the middle of the 1960's the argument for the unity of authorship of Chronicles, Ezra, and Nehemiah appeared to have triumphed in very convincing fashion. That these books were the work of a single author had been the dominant opinion since it was proposed by Leopold Zunz in the 1830's.[1] The one notable, early exception to this view was Adam C. Welch.[2]

---

[1]Leopold Zunz, *Die Gottes dienstlichen Vorträge der Juden, historisch Entwickelt: Ein Beitrag zur Alternumskunde und Biblischen Kritik, zur Literatur und Religionsgeschichte* (Berlin: A. Asher, 1832), p. 19.

[2]Adam C. Welch, *Post-Exilic Judaism* (London: William Blackwood & Sons, 1935), p. 193.

Throughout the history of the development of this argument a variety of points have been used to make a case for unity or disunity. These may be summarized as follows.

First, II Chronicles and Ezra appear to be linked together by the decree of Cyrus which appears in both books. Peter R. Ackroyd asserted that these shared verses are ". . . a clear directive to the reader that it is to Ezra and Nehemiah he should move after Chronicles."[3] Welch went the other direction with this same piece of evidence, maintaining that no person would bother to link two works together in this way unless they had originally been separate.[4] This dispute has raged on until the present including a specific debate between Menahem Haran, who presupposes the unity of Chronicles and Ezra and Hugh Williamson, one of the strongest proponents for disunity. Haran has argued that the books are connected by catch-lines because together they were too long to fit on one scroll. He pointed to the analogous separations in the Pentateuch, saying that catch-lines were not needed there because the breaks came at natural divisions in the narrative.[5] Williamson effectively destroyed these arguments. There is no evidence concerning the length of scrolls, and as for the presence or absence of natural breaks in the narrative, what better division could there be than the Exile itself? Instead, Williamson proposed three other reasons for the overlap, all of which involve the borrowing of the decree from the beginning of Ezra and placing it on the end of Chronicles. This may have been done by the author of Chronicles to add a note of hope to the end of the narrative, or by the worshipping community as a common liturgical practice for the same reason, or by a later

---

[3]Peter R. Ackroyd, "Chronicles-Ezra-Nehemiah: The Concept of Unity," *ZAW*, 100 (1988 Supplement), 193.

[4]Welch, *Post-Exilic*, p. 186.

[5]Menahem Haran, "Explaining the Identical Lines at the End of Chronicles and the Beginning of Ezra," *BRev*, 2 (1986), 19.

editor to point readers to the continuation of Israel's history.[6] This phenomenon fails to provide proof for unity or disunity. It is easy enough to explain the existence of overlapping lines from either point of view.

A second issue concerning the relationship of Chronicles and Ezra is the placement of the books within the canon. The order of the books in the LXX certainly indicates that they were placed chronologically at a very early stage. Because the textual history of the LXX is such a mystery, it is impossible to determine when its ordering became an acceptable alternative to that of the Hebrew Bible. Whatever the process, it was apparent to some persons in ancient times that Chronicles ought to precede Ezra and Nehemiah. Perhaps the more puzzling question is why the order of the Hebrew Bible was maintained with Chronicles at the very end of the canon. The simplest answer is that the standard for order in the Hebrew canon was authority. The books of Ezra and Nehemiah, along with all of the prophetic books, were accorded greater authority because of the personal names attached to them. The Greek canon made use of some other criteria, chronology being one of them.[7] This line of argument also fails to prove or disprove unity of authorship. It does establish an early tradition of placing the books in a chronological relationship.

A third problem is the existence of I Esdras. This apocryphal work consists of the last two chapters of II Chronicles, all of Ezra, and Nehemiah 7:72-8:13. Opinions vary widely as to the character of I Esdras. One extreme

---

[6]H. G. M. Williamson, "Did the Author of Chronicles also Write the Books of Ezra and Nehemiah?," *BRev*, 3 (1987), 56-59. See also Williamson's [*Israel in the Books of Chronicles* (London: Cambridge University Press, 1977), p. 8] discussion of this issue in greater detail including the work of H. Hunger (*Babylonische und Assyriche Kolophone*, Alter Orient und Altes Testament, vol. 2 [Neukirchen-Vluyn: Nukirchener Verlag, 1968], p. 1). Hunger documented the use of a *Stichzeile* in Babylonian literature. This device consists of overlapping lines at the end of one tablet and the beginning of the next in a long, continuous text. Still, however, there is no evidence of the use of this type of device anywhere else in the Hebrew Bible.

[7]Simon J. DeVries, *1 and 2 Chronicles* (Grand Rapids, Michigan: Wm. B. Eerdmans Publishing Co., 1989), p. 10.

was expressed by Charles C. Torrey, who insisted that it was not an intentional work of an author or compiler at all. Rather, it is merely a fragment from the Old Greek version of the work of the Chronicler.[8] Aside from assuming the unity of authorship of Chronicles, Ezra, and Nehemiah, this view also depends upon a theoretical, original Greek text to explain the differences between I Esdras and the extant versions of the LXX. A quite opposite position has been taken by H. W. Attridge, who has argued that I Esdras was ". . . designed to play some role in the polemic of the second century between the Jerusalem temple and its rivals."[9] This was accomplished by excising the necessary portions from all three books to demonstrate the continuity of the second temple with that of Solomon. Such a process might account for the alterations in the text without appealing to an unknown *Vorlage.* Once again, unity of authorship is neither proved nor disproved. I Esdras does represent an early tradition which viewed the narrative of Chronicles and Ezra as continuous and made use of them as such. The reliance of Josephus upon I Esdras alone for his record of the Exile and Restoration establishes the influence of this tradition.

A final, and most complex area of dispute is the alleged presence of, or lack of, continuity in vocabulary, style, and important themes between the two works. In the late nineteenth century, following the lead of Zunz and others, S. R. Driver compiled an extensive list of vocabulary and stylistic elements unique to Chronicles, Ezra, and Nehemiah.[10] As Williamson has

---

[8]Charles C. Torrey, "A Revised View of I Esdras," in *Louis Ginzberg Jubilee Volume* (New York: Academy for Jewish Research, 1945), p. 395. See also Jacob M. Myers (*I and II Esdras,* AB [Garden City, New York: Doubleday & Co., 1974], pp. 5-6) for a discussion of the possible origins of I Esdras including: (1) It is a compiled narrative from the LXX of Chronicles, Ezra, and Nehemiah, (2) it is merely a portion of an early Greek text, or (3) it is a translation of a text originally extant in Hebrew.

[9]H. W. Attridge, "Historiography," in *Jewish Writings of the Second Temple Period* (Philadelphia: Fortress Press, 1984), p. 160.

[10]S. R. Driver, *An Introduction to the Literature of the Old Testament* (Edinburgh: T & T Clark, 1913), pp. 535-540.

pointed out, the intent of this list was not to establish unity of authorship, but to present some observations about the literature of the post-Exilic era. This list and others like it, however, came to be used by others as evidence of unity.[11] Common vocabulary and style can be the result of a variety of factors, common authorship being only one possibility. The books may simply have emerged from the same specific time period and geographic setting. They could have both been the product of a particular community. The writer of one may even have used the other as a reference, inadvertently or intentionally borrowing vocabulary and stylistic elements.

The opposite direction on this issue was taken up by Sara Japhet in the late 1960's. She compiled a very intricate list of linguistic evidence highlighting the differences between Chronicles and Ezra-Nehemiah.[12] Williamson continued this effort over the next decade, thoroughly dismantling the lists compiled by Driver and Curtis and Madsen.[13] His conclusion, however, was not that disunity had been proved; but that the evidence for unity had been removed, returning the burden of proof to those arguing for unity.[14]

The problem of comparing and contrasting themes, theology, or ideology is even more slippery. To begin with, two books having similar interests is certainly no proof that they were written by the same author. On the other hand, there is no reason why one author could not write two books with divergent interests. There have been a large number of proposed primary themes for the books of Chronicles. A more thorough discussion of

---

[11]H. G. M. Williamson, *Israel in the Books of Chronicles* (London: Cambridge University Press, 1977), p. 38.

[12]Sara Japhet, "The Supposed Common Authorship of Chronicles and Ezra Investigated Anew," *VT*, 18 (1969), 334-370. Perhaps the simplest and clearest example of the type of evidence Japhet cited is the careful consistency in the spelling of proper names in Ezra and Nehemiah compared to the frequent inconsistency in Chronicles (p. 341).

[13]Williamson, *Israel*, pp. 37-59.

[14]Ibid., p. 59.

the theology of the Chronicler will appear in a later section. The following is just a brief example of how the issue can be used as an argument for or against unity. One of the most frequent suggestions is that the Chronicler's main concern is the correctness and purity of cultic activity within the temple. This is certainly a primary concern in Ezra and Nehemiah as well. Of course, it is obvious that this in no way proves that these books were produced by the same author. On the other hand, James D. Newsome has listed several important themes from Chronicles which are absent from Ezra and Nehemiah: (1) Kings function as prophets in Chronicles, but not so in Ezra or Nehemiah, (2) in Chronicles the temple is open to foreigners while Ezra and Nehemiah are highly exclusive, (3) God is presented as a manipulator of events in Chronicles, yet God does not exhibit such control in Ezra and Nehemiah, and (4) Chronicles contains future hope for the Davidic kingship while Ezra and Nehemiah do not.[15] It is not difficult to respond to any of these arguments. For example, how could kings function as prophets in Ezra and Nehemiah when there were no kings. Nevertheless, these thematic arguments against unity seemed to gain momentum through the 1970's and 1980's.

Recently, however, Joseph Blenkinsopp has raised some questions about the conclusiveness of the arguments for disunity.[16] Most importantly for this study, Blenkinsopp has highlighted the literary continuity created by the parallel sequence of reform movements followed by the celebration of Passover in Chronicles and the rebuilding of the temple followed by a passover celebration in Ezra. He has identified in these common elements ". . . a unity of concept which binds together the two works into one history

---

[15]James D. Newsome, "Toward a New Understanding of the Chronicler and His Purposes," *JBL*, 94 (1975), 203-213. This list is one example of the types of contrasts which have been produced. See also Williamson, *Israel*, pp. 60-69.

[16]Joseph Blenkinsopp, *Ezra-Nehemiah*, OTL (Philadelphia: Westminster Press, 1988), pp. 49-53.

with its own distinctive point of view and purpose."[17]

This study will not assume that a conclusive argument for unity can be made. The end of Chronicles and beginning of Ezra will be read together as a continuous narrative, however, for a few important reasons. First, the overlapping lines, the order of the Greek text, and the existence of I Esdras indicate at least that they have been read together by some persons and in some traditions for over 2000 years. Second, the Christian canon places them together in this way. As long as unity remains a debatable issue,[18] attempts should be made to read Chronicles and Ezra together to determine whether fruitful results might be obtained from this method of interpretation.

Another issue somewhat related to the unity debate is how the texts of Chronicles, Ezra, and Nehemiah acquired their current form. Included in this area of investigation is the analysis of the use of sources in these books. The textual history of the Hebrew Bible is extremely complex and mysterious. Chronicles, Ezra, and Nehemiah are not exceptions to this pattern. In fact the high level of complexity and uncertainty in this area may serve as an argument for a multiplicity of readings, including the one proposed in this study.

Frank M. Cross has offered what is probably the most influential reconstruction of the textual history of Chronicles, Ezra, and Nehemiah. Cross proposed that the original work of the Chronicler, written in about 520 B.C.E., began at I Chronicles 10 and went through Ezra 3:13. This work was a polemic for the restoration of Zerubbabel. The second stage of development was the addition of the rest of Ezra around 458. The final edition, the present canonical form, added the genealogies in I Chronicles 1-9

---

[17]Ibid., p. 54.

[18]Williamson, "Did the Author . . . ," p. 56. In his most recent comments on the subject Williamson has called the argument a "wide open question."

and the Nehemiah Memoirs sometime around 400.[19] The dependence of this reconstruction on a supposed *Vorlage* of I Esdras is one of its several weaknesses.[20]

Additional support for a proposed early edition of Chronicles has come from Paul D. Hanson. Hanson seized this work as evidence for his Zadokite restoration hypothesis, citing the Chronicler's preoccupation with the ordering of temple personnel as evidence that the written work was present at the time of rebuilding.[21] Writing slightly earlier than Cross, David N. Freedman argued that the first edition of Chronicles was written just after the completion of the temple in about 515. Freedman extended the scope of this original work through Ezra 6, but did not include the Aramaic portion presently found in Ezra 4:6-6:18. This addition would include the dedication of the new temple and the celebration of Passover at the end of chapter 6.[22]

The relatively simple solutions above tend to avoid a few complex, critical issues including the use of sources within the large blocks of material and the relationship between Chronicles and the MT version of the Deuteronomistic History. A thorough analysis of the textual history of this material would require an intricate examination of smaller portions of the text. Recently, Baruch Halpern has attempted to describe the complex redactional history of Ezra 1-6.[23] In his conclusion Halpern compared the

---

[19]Frank M. Cross, "A Reconstruction of the Judean Restoration," *JBL*, 94 (1975), 13-15.

[20]Any thorough reconstruction necessarily relies upon specific conclusions concerning very debatable issues. This particular proposal assumes not only the unity of authorship of Chronicles and part of Ezra, but also the early date for Ezra's work (458), an issue which will be discussed in a later section.

[21]Paul D. Hanson, *The People Called* (New York: Harper & Row, 1986), pp. 263-264.

[22]David N. Freedman, "The Chronicler's Purpose," *CBQ*, 23 (1961), 441.

[23]Baruch Halpern, "A Historiographical Commentary on Ezra 1-6," in *The Hebrew Bible and its Interpreters*, ed. William Henry Propp, et al. (Winona Lake, Indiana: Eisenbrauns, 1990), pp. 81-142. Halpern's convoluted reordering of Ezra 3:1-6 (p. 94) is just one example of the enormous complexities involved in this process.

use of sources in Chronicles with the use of sources in Ezra 1-6, and he found the methodology to be quite different. Whereas the Chronicler often revised the sequence of events portrayed in the Deuteronomistic History to suit his purposes, the author of Ezra 1-6 chose a more timeless approach, removing the emphasis on the chronology of events altogether.[24]

Farther in the background of the development of these texts is the nature of the sources used by the authors. A discussion of the sources used by the writer of Chronicles must begin with the Deuteronomistic History. It is clear that the author used a version of Samuel and Kings as the primary source. At times Chronicles repeats the Samuel/Kings material verbatim. At other times, however, the author deleted from, added to, paraphrased, or rearranged the earlier history. There is no clear pattern of consistency. Surprisingly, the text of Chronicles is much closer to its parallels in Samuel than in Kings.[25] A common mistake in the past has been to find in every divergence a clue to the Chronicler's purpose or theology. Werner Lemke undercut this practice with his demonstration that the Hebrew Chronicles often agrees with the LXX of Samuel against the MT of Samuel. This observation would indicate that the Chronicler used a *Vorlage* of Samuel quite different from the present text in the Hebrew Bible.[26] The evidence from

---

[24]Ibid., pp. 131-134. The author of Ezra 1-6, for example, refused to solve the Sheshbazzar/Zerubbabel problem by combining or reordering the events. Instead, he placed them side by side with no emphasis of chronological sequence. It should be noted that even if Halpern's argument here is correct, it does not necessarily support the case for the disunity of the two works. There is no reason why a single author could not have made very different use of two very different sets of source material.

[25]Wilson I. Chang, "The *Tendenz* of the Chronicler" (Ph.D. dissertation, Hartford Theological Seminary, 1973), p. 16.

[26]Werner Lemke, "The Synoptic Problem in the Chronicler's History," *HTR*, 58 (1965), 362. The Greek text of Chronicles (*Paraleipomenon*) has been a source of interesting debate itself. Leslie C. Allen [*The Greek Chronicles: The Relation of the Septuagint of I and II Chronicles to the MT. Part II: Textual Transmission*, supplements to *VT*, vol. 27 (Leiden: E. J. Brill, 1974), pp. 167-168.] debunked Torrey's contention that *Paraleipomenon* was a second century C.E. Theodotian work. Instead, he established that the Greek text reflects a Hebrew text of second century B.C.E. Egyptian origin, which is very close to MT.

Qumran provides further support for this contention. In many instances where Chronicles appears to part from the MT of Samuel, the text of Chronicles actually agrees more closely with the Samuel scrolls from Cave four.[27] While the Qumran witnesses to Kings are too fragmentary to provide a definite conclusion, it is logical to assume that such a pattern would continue.[28]

Most important for this study are Steven McKenzie's observations about the Chronicler's use of the Deuteronomistic source. According to McKenzie's analysis the Chronicler followed Samuel and Kings closely when using them, showing his hand most clearly in the omissions, such as the removal of any negative evaluations of Solomon.[29] This pattern ends abruptly, however, after II Chronicles 28. The material in II Chronicles 29-36, which reports Judah's history from the reign of Hezekiah to the fall of Jerusalem, is unique to the Chronicler. McKenzie's explanation is that the Chronicler made use of Dtr1, a product of the Josianic Reform and not Dtr2, an exilic extension of the Deuteronomistic History.[30]

If the author of Chronicles frequently parted from the Deuteronomistic History, even to the point of adding seven chapters at the end, it might be reasonable to assume that he used other sources. No hard evidence of any

---

[27]See examples in Frank M. Cross, *The Ancient Library at Qumran and Modern Biblical Studies* (Garden City, New York: Doubleday & Co., 1961), p. 188. See also Cross, "The History of the Biblical Text in the Light of the Discoveries in the Judean Desert," *HTR*, 57 (1964), 284. Here Cross contended that 4QSamb agrees with the LXX thirteen times while the reverse phenomenon occurs only four times

[28]Three sets of fragments were found in Caves Four, Five, and Six. 4QKgs, containing at least part of I Kings 7 and 8, is not yet available for study. 5QKgs is fragmentary but does contain one sizable section of about fifteen lines of I Kings 1 with three to four words per line. While a full comparison is impossible, all of these words appear in MT, making close agreement likely. Most of the fragments of 6QKgs are one word or less. Only a portion of the Elisha narrative of II Kings 7 is of any substance. The lack of a parallel makes any comparison with Chronicles against MT Kings impossible.

[29]Steven L. McKenzie, *The Chronicler's Use of the Deuteronomic History* (Atlanta: Scholar's Press, 1984), p. 113.

[30]Ibid., p. 187.

such sources has been found, however.[31] At the same time the opposite argument that all additions or changes are the creation of the author of Chronicles is without positive proof.

Firm conclusions about the use of sources in the composition of Ezra and Nehemiah are even more difficult to draw. Even a casual reading of the two books reveals the literary and historical problems in the text. An obvious example is the intrusion of Ezra material at Nehemiah 8:10. Such observations have led to numerous attempts to reorder the two books. For years the most influential of these was Torrey's.[32] Recent proposals range from Karl Friedrich Pohlmann's placement of Nehemiah 8 at the end of Ezra 1-10 as the original extension of Chronicles[33] to Williamson's claim that the sources for Ezra 7-Nehemiah 11 were all written at about the time of the events themselves compiled about 400 B.C.E. in their present order. The end of Nehemiah was added just slightly later and Ezra 1-6 after about a century.[34] Most important for this study are the observations of Blenkinsopp[35] and Williamson,[36] begrudgingly, that Ezra 1-6 may have very close affinities to Chronicles.

The proposals defining the theology, purpose, or primary themes of

---

[31]Robert North, "Does Archaeology Prove Chronicle's Sources?," in *A Light unto My Path: Old Testament Studies in Honor of Jacob M. Myers*, ed. Howard N. Bream, et al. Philadelphia: Temple University (Philadelphia: Temple University Press, 1974), p. 392.

[32]Charles C. Torrey, *Ezra Studies* (New York: Ktav Publishing, 1970), pp. 252-258. Torrey's reordering of the text was Ezra 1-8, Nehemiah 7:70-8:18, Ezra 9-10, Nehemiah 9-10, Nehemiah 1-7, Nehemiah 11-13.

[33]Karl Friedrich Pohlmann, *Studien zum Dritten Esra: Ein Beitrag zur Frage nach dem ursprünglichen Schluss des Chronisten Geschichteswerkes* (Göttingen: Vanderhoeck und Ruprecht, 1970), pp. 127-131. Pohlmann's movement of Nehemiah 8 is based at least partly upon the text of I Esdras. See his statement of the problem of I Esdras on pp. 14-15.

[34]H. G. M. Williamson, *Ezra-Nehemiah*, WBC (Waco, Texas: Word Publishing, 1985), pp. xxxv-xxxvi.

[35]Blenkinsopp, *Ezra-Nehemiah*, p. 44.

[36]H. G. M. Williamson, "The Composition of Ezra i-iv," *JTS*, 33 (1983), 1-30.

Chronicles are about as numerous as its interpreters.[37]   As mentioned earlier, most interpreters recognize a preoccupation with the Jerusalem cult as at least a major theme. Within this broad category is the effort to establish the legitimate role of the Levites. The overall goal is to unite all of Israel in proper worship in the tradition of David.[38] For the writer of Chronicles the temple cult was a vital source of continuity with pre-Exilic Israel.

The author of Chronicles was obviously intensely interested in the Davidic kingship. From the point of view presented in Chronicles, the monarchy was divinely ordained and the kingdom of Israel was equated with the kingdom of God. Williamson has pointed out divergences from the Deuteronomistic History which illustrate this point, such as the alteration of "your house" and "your kingdom" in II Samuel 7:16 to "my house" and "my kingdom" in I Chronicles 13:8.[39]

Rudolf Mosis has highlighted the use of the monarchy as an overall pattern by the Chronicler. He asserted that the monarchy in Chronicles follows an alternating structure of exile and restoration. Solomon is set up as an ultimate ideal. The kings following Solomon are patterned after either Saul or David in alternating reversals of destruction and salvation.[40]   In forming this pattern for his audience, the Chronicler's primary purpose was to proclaim the need to turn back to Yahweh.[41]

---

[37]For an exhaustive list see Chang, "The *Tendenz* . . . ," pp. 12-13.

[38]Roddy Braun, "The Message of Chronicles: Rally Round the Temple," *CTM*, 42 (1971), 512.

[39]H. G. M. Williamson, *1 and 2 Chronicles*, NCBC (Grand Rapids, Michigan: Wm. B. Eerdmans Publishing, 1982), p. 26.

[40]Rudolf Mosis *Unterschungen zur Theologie des chronisten Geschichteswerkes* (Freiburg: Herder, 1973), pp. 186-189, 203-204. Mosis pointed to I Chronicles 10, the first passage following the genealogies, as the starting point for this pattern (pp. 28-41). I Chronicles 13-14 pointedly describes Saul's unfaithfulness, Saul's rejection by Yahweh, and David's subsequent rise to the throne. Later, Manasseh would serve as a complete model of exile and restoration in his own apostasy and repentence (pp. 192-194).

[41]Ibid., p. 202.

A third theme commonly identified in Chronicles is retribution. Though this is sometimes referred to as immediate retribution, Robert North's description of "short range retribution" is probably more accurate since God's judgment was frequently delayed by positive action.[42] Nevertheless, it was always imminent.

The themes of Chronicles can take on an altered meaning if Ezra and Nehemiah are considered a natural extension of the work. James D. Newsome has outlined a synthesis of the three most vital components of Israelite religion within this record of Israel's history. Prophecy, kingdom, and cult were brought together in the late sixth century B.C.E. in the prophetic work of Haggai and Zachariah and the building activity of the Davidide, Zerubbabel, which culminated in the founding of the new temple.[43] If this merging of the central institutions of Israel actually took place then it was a very short-lived phenomenon, as the hope of a restored Davidic monarchy seems to fade from the pages of Ezra and Nehemiah.

Roddy Braun has summed up the apparent theological differences between Chronicles and Ezra-Nehemiah. In addition to the fading of the monarchy's importance,[44] the emphasis in Chronicles on inclusiveness and retribution is also missing from Ezra-Nehemiah. In Chronicles the citizens of the former northern kingdom are frequently included in the religious life of Judah. Ezra-Nehemiah, on the other hand shows frequent hostility toward northerners and foreigners.[45] Chronicles also portrays divine retribution towards those who are unfaithful, while Ezra-Nehemiah places much greater

---

[42]Robert North, "The Theology of the Chronicler," *JBL*, 82 (1963), 367.

[43]James D. Newsome, "Toward a New Understanding of the Chronicler and His Purposes," *JBL*, 94 (1975), 215-216.

[44]Roddy L. Braun, "Chronicles, Ezra, and Nehemiah: Theological and Literary History," in vol. 30 of Supplements to *VT* (Leiden: E. J. Brill, 1979), p. 61.

[45]Ibid., pp. 56-57.

emphasis on God's mercy.[46]

Most important for this study is the Chronicler's emphasis on cult, a theme which is obviously continued in Ezra and Nehemiah. While this has received much attention, little notice has been focused upon the act of sacrifice within the events narrated in this history.

A difficult historical problem has arisen, as critical study of Ezra and Nehemiah has been conducted. Ezra 7:8 reports that Ezra came to Jerusalem in the seventh year of Artaxerxes. Nehemiah 2:1 places Nehemiah's return in the twentieth year of Artaxerxes. The first problem with arriving at the simple conclusion that Nehemiah arrived in Jerusalem thirteen years after Ezra is that there were two kings of this name in that era, Artaxerxes I (465-424) and Artaxerxes II (405-358). While it may be rather remarkable that the texts of Ezra and Nehemiah evolved in such a way as to make reference to two different kings without differentiating between them, this possibility offers a solution to a number of problems and, of course, creates some others.

The reverse chronology of Ezra and Nehemiah, placing the latter first, was made popular by A. van Hoonaker during the end of the nineteenth century and the first quarter of the twentieth century. This reversal is made possible by the relatively simple assumption that Ezra returned during the seventh year of Artaxerxes II (398) while Nehemiah had already returned during the twentieth year of Artaxerxes I (445).[47] Of course, such a reversal not only changes their order, but also widens the gap between their arrival significantly. A forty-seven year gap makes it highly unlikely that the two were both alive and in Jerusalem at the same time, much less in the active portions of their careers simultaneously.

The arguments in favor of reversal were summed up at the middle of

---

[46]Ibid., pp. 53-55.

[47]A. van Hoonaker, "La succession chronologique Néhémie-Esdras," *RB*, 32, (1923), pp. 31-32.

the nineteenth century by H. H. Rowley.[48] The first of these arguments is that according to Ezra 9:9 Ezra arrived in Jerusalem to find the wall already built.[49] Thus, the primary work of Nehemiah appears to have already been accomplished. Second, it is apparent, in verses like Ezra 10:1, that during the time of Ezra the land was reasonably well populated; while Nehemiah 7:4 portrays a sparsely populated Jerusalem.[50] Third, Nehemiah's name precedes Ezra's in Nehemiah 12:6.[51] Fourth, Nehemiah's activity coincides with the high priesthood of Eliashib (Nehemiah 3:1) and Ezra's with that of Jehohanan (Ezra 10:6). Though it is debatable, Jehohanan appears to be either Eliashib's son or grandson.[52]

The fifth argument involves the complex use of a letter from Egypt to date the work of Ezra and Nehemiah. Dates established in the late fifth century letter from Elephantine place Johanan (=Jehohanan) as high priest around 410 and the twilight of Sanballat's governorship at about the same time. Based on these dates the high priesthood of Eliashib and the high point of Sanballat's term could be pushed back toward the middle of the fifth century during the reign of Artaxerxes I. All of this would solidify the assignment of Nehemiah's career to the reign of Artaxerxes I, while placing Ezra's activity in the late fifth and early fourth centuries during the reign of Artaxerxes II.[53]

The sixth argument is that Ezra goes unmentioned for most of the

---

[48]H. H. Rowley, "The Chronological Order of Ezra and Nehemiah," in *Ignace Goldziher Memorial Volume*, vol. 1, ed. D. S. Lowinger and J. Somogyi (Budapest: Globus, 1948), pp. 127-140. Rowley also provided extensive lists of van Hoonaker's supporters (pp. 120-121) and detractors (p. 120).

[49]Ibid., p. 127.

[50]Ibid., p. 131.

[51]Ibid., p. 132.

[52]Ibid., pp. 133-134.

[53]Ibid., pp. 135-138.

book of Nehemiah, which would make sense if Ezra came second.[54] Finally, in Nehemiah 13:13, Nehemiah appointed temple treasurers. According to Ezra 8:33, when Ezra arrived in Jerusalem there were already persons holding this office.[55]

There are two other alternatives for solving some of the chronological problems of Ezra and Nehemiah. The first involves a simple emendation of Ezra 7:8 to place Ezra after Nehemiah with both still in the reign of Artaxerxes I. Rowley was correct in labelling such emendations as "purely conjectural."[56] More influential has been Torrey's contention that Ezra was a purely fictional character. Torrey described Ezra as something of an alter ego of the Chronicler, who he believed wrote the entire Ezra narrative, projected into the story of the Restoration to articulate the Chronicler's concerns.[57] While this proposal has a certain appeal, it is tied too closely to the unity of authorship position, and is without any hard evidence.

Since Rowley's masterful summation, debate on this issue has continued.[58] Williamson has advanced some newer arguments in favor of the early date for Ezra (458). First, he placed the priority on the order of events as presented in the Bible, and put the burden of proof upon any other proposal.[59] Second, Nehemiah's dealings with what seems to be a very local problem with mixed marriages (Nehemiah 13:23-28) make more sense if they follow the broader reforms of Ezra.[60] Third, the reforms of Nehemiah 10

---

[54]Ibid., p. 141.

[55]Ibid., p. 142.

[56]Ibid., p. 123.

[57]Torrey, *Ezra Studies*, pp. 242-246.

[58]For a list of some more recent advocates and opponents of the reverse chronology see H. G. M. Williamson, *Ezra-Nehemiah*, p. xl.

[59]Ibid., pp. xlii-xliii.

[60]Ibid., p. xliii.

appear to be based on those of Ezra in Nehemiah 13.[61] Fourth, the similarity between the purposes of Ezra and Nehemiah indicate that one was completing the failed attempt of the other. The governmental authority that Nehemiah carried made it more likely that he was the successful second reformer.[62] Finally, because the reference to Ezra at the dedication of the wall in Nehemiah 12:36 provides literary symmetry to the narrative, it is probably original to the text, placing Ezra and Nehemiah at the same event.[63] For these and other reasons, Williamson dated the arrival of Ezra to the seventh year of Artaxerxes I (458).[64]

Blenkinsopp also opted for the early date of Ezra, though less vehemently, asserting that if the compiler wished to create an artificial order he would have more likely put Ezra second, emphasizing his work as the crowning achievement. The failure of the compiler to do so probably indicates that the actual chronology of events was too well known to alter.[65]

No proposed date for Ezra can be sustained with conclusive evidence, though the arguments for the reverse chronology are certainly less subjective than those for the order presented in the text. For the purposes of this study it is important to note that these literary accounts present, first and foremost, a theological interpretation of the Exile and Restoration. If it could be proved that the compiler took serious liberties with the chronology of events, then important theological inferences might be drawn. The mere observation that the author did not produce a carefully documented historical record, as is indicated by the content of the arguments above, is a strong indication that the primary motive of the compiler was to make statements about the nature

---

[61]Ibid.

[62]Ibid., p. xliv.

[63]Ibid.

[64]Ibid.

[65]Blenkinsopp, *Ezra-Nehemiah*, p. 144.

of the restored community and its religious life.

Summary

An attempt has been made here to outline the vital issues in the study of Chronicles, Ezra, and Nehemiah, and to link those issues with the intended course of this study. The issue of unity of authorship has important implications, but, as the above discussion reveals, firm conclusions are impossible. Likewise, the textual history remains much of a mystery, and poses the added difficulty of dating this material as a whole or as component parts. The purpose and theology of the authors of Chronicles, Ezra, and Nehemiah cannot be neatly categorized or summed up under a single idea. It is likely that their purposes are many. The intent of this chapter has been to provide a historical-critical backdrop for the discussion to follow. Further background will be provided on more detailed points as the need arises. In addition, the reader will be referred back from time to time to the discussion presented in this chapter.

Though the material presented in this chapter indicates that extensive work has been done on Chronicles, Ezra, and Nehemiah, there has yet to be a thorough discussion on the function of sacrifice in these books. In fact, much of the recent literature has given the issue little or no attention. Therefore, while this study is related to, and dependent upon, prior research such as that already presented, it will be argued that a new focus may provide fresh interpretive results without necessarily assuming any particular position concerning the issues discussed above.

Chapter 2

SACRIFICIAL EVENTS IN II CHRONICLES

Before turning to specific texts in Chronicles, it will be helpful to take a brief look at some of the issues involved in the interpretation of these books. Some of this material was discussed in the opening chapter, and will be reviewed and elaborated upon here and throughout this chapter, as necessary.

Questions concerning the date of Chronicles are not easily answered. The proposal of Cross, outlined in chapter one of this study, would date all the portions of Chronicles relevant to this chapter in the late sixth century.[66] Cross, Freedman, Hanson, and others have interpreted Chronicles as part of a program for the restoration of Israel. If this is so, then it must have emerged in the early years after the return from exile, before the Restoration had developed significantly. Many scholars, including those who have contended for the unity of Chronicles and Ezra as well as some who have not, placed the date of Chronicles much later.[67] The assumption that the ministries of Ezra and Nehemiah were accomplished when Chronicles was compiled would push the date down to the late fifth or early fourth century. The intense desire to interpret the Exile, as well as to establish lines of

---

[66]Frank M. Cross, "A Reconstruction of the Judean Restoration," *JBL*, 94 (1975), 13-15.

[67]For an example see W. A. L. Elmslie, "The First and Second Books of Chronicles," *IB*, vol. 3, ed. George Buttrick (Nashville: Abingdon, 1954), pp. 345-347. On the basis of linguistic arguments and inferences about conflict within the priesthood, Elmslie assumed a date between 450 and 350.

continuity with the pre-Exilic cult, hardly seems fitting a century or more after the temple was rebuilt. Therefore, this study will proceed on the assumption that the essential portions of Chronicles emerged during the late sixth century.[68] This is not a dogmatic conclusion based on irrefutable evidence, but a working hypothesis for the interpretation to follow.

The authorship of Chronicles is a question about which it is even more difficult to take a firm position. II Chronicles 36:20 would indicate that the author's loyalties lay with the returned community. On this basis, the author would seem to be a member of, or a descendent of a member of, the returned community; and a person closely tied to the Jerusalem cult. The emphasis on the role of the Levites begs the conclusion that he was a Levite. It is enough to say that he was closely identified with this clerical community.[69] Again, it awaits to be seen whether this assumption will lend to the interpretation to follow, and whether the interpretation confirms such a position about authorship.

All but one of the texts discussed in this chapter are from II Chronicles 29-36. Therefore, a brief outline of those eight chapters is in order here:

I.   Hezekiah's Reform and Cleansing of the Temple (29:1-36).

II.   Hezekiah's Passover (30:1-27).

III. Hezekiah's Organization of the Temple (31:1-21).

IV.   Assyrian Attack and God's Rescue of Judah (32:1-23).

V.   Hezekiah's Illness and Death (32:24-33).

VI.   The Reign of Mannasseh (33:1-20).

VII. The Reign of Amon (33:21-25).

---

[68]Whether or not portions such as I Chronicles 1-9 were later additions has little or no bearing on this study.

[69]While this discussion refers to the Chronicler as an individual, it is quite possible that a small group of scribes produced Chronicles. From this point forward the use of the term "Chronicler" will allow for that possibility. The use of male pronouns to designate the author of Chronicles is not the result of subconscious male bias; but a conclusion, based on an understanding of the era and the text, that the author of Chronicles was male.

Elaborate descriptions of sacrificial events are not abundant in Chronicles. There are several prominent events; however, most of these appear at the end of II Chronicles. Solomon's temple dedication in II Chronicles is a significant exception. Though the details are sparse when compared to later events, it may have served as an important reference for some of the later accounts. This chapter will also include an analysis of the passages describing Hezekiah's reform, Hezekiah's passover, Josiah's reform, Josiah's passover, and the destruction of Judah. The main line of argument will be that Chronicles becomes preoccupied with sacrifice as the Exile approaches, leading up to a bloody climax in II Chronicles 36:17 when the young people of Israel were slaughtered in the temple by the Babylonians as the ultimate act of purification.

Solomon's Dedication of the Temple
II Chronicles 7:1-10

1 When Solomon finished praying the fire came down from heaven and consumed the burnt offering and the sacrifices; and the glory of the Lord filled the house.2 But the priests were not able to go unto the house of the Lord,[70] for the glory of the Lord filled the house of the Lord. 3 All the sons of Israel saw when the fire came down and the glory of the Lord was about the house. They bowed, faces to the ground, upon the stones, and they worshiped, giving thanks to the Lord:

For he is good,

---

[70]LXX adds "at that time."

For his mercy is forever.

4 The king and all the people performed sacrifices before the Lord. 5 And the king, Solomon, sacrificed a sacrifice: the oxen - 22,000, and sheep - 120,000. 6 The priests were standing upon their places, and the Levites, with all the instruments of the music of the Lord which David the king made to give thanks to the Lord; for to eternity is his mercy when David praised by their hand. The priests were sounding trumpets before them and all Israel stood. 7 Solomon sanctified the midst of the court which was before the house of the Lord; for there he offered the burnt offerings and the fat portions of the offerings of well-being, for the altar of bronze which Solomon made was not able to hold the burnt offerings, the grain offering, and the fat portions. 8 Solomon held the festival at that time seven days, and all Israel with him, a very great assembly from Lebo Hamath to the Wadi of Egypt. 9 On the eighth day they conducted a solemn assembly. For the dedication of the altar they had performed for seven days and the festival seven days. 10 On the twenty-third day of the seventh month he sent the people to their tents, joyful and in good heart about the good which the Lord had done for David and for Solomon and for his people Israel.

The sacrifices at Solomon's dedication of the temple followed his lengthy prayer in the previous chapter. There is significant confusion in the flow of the larger narrative. II Chronicles 5:6 reports that innumerable sheep and oxen were being sacrificed as the ark was being brought to the temple. Suddenly at 7:1 a previously unmentioned sacrifice is consumed by fire from heaven. In 7:4 Solomon and the people are again offering sacrifices of oxen (22,000) and sheep (120,000). In addition, II Chronicles 5:13-14 parallels 7:1-3 very closely. Both report that God's presence filled the temple , and, therefore, the priests were unable to carry out their duties.

The Chronicler's report of these events follows that of I Kings 8, the glaring exception being the second appearance of the glory of the Lord in II Chronicles 7:1-3. Why are there two appearances of the cloud? Is all of this part of the original work or have there been later additions? One typical answer to such questions is that 7:1-4 is a later addition to the text while 5:13-

14 is genuine.[71]   Of course, there is the opposite position that 7:1-4 is authentic and 5:13-14 is the intrusion.[72]   Raymond B. Dillard has proposed a literary structure for the whole of II Chronicles 1-9 which answers these questions without carving up the text.   These nine chapters appear to be a great chiasm of Solomonic activity with Solomon's speeches to the people (6:1-11) and to God (6:12-42) forming the central, reflected element. The appearance of the glory cloud in 7:1-3, therefore, simply mirrors the event in 5:13-14.   In the same way the sacrifices in 5:6 and 7:4-5 are matching accounts.[73]

There are two peculiarities which this literary structure does not explain.   First, why is the sacrificial episode in 7:4-5 slightly more detailed than that in 5:6?   One answer, of course, is that they are both duplicates of the Kings material (I Kings 8:5 and 8:62-63 respectively); but this just moves the question back one step.   5:6 is little more than an off-hand remark about the ark processional.   7:4-5 gives the actual number of animals sacrificed, a number that is very large.[74]   This may not seem to be a terribly important point, but the difference in the two reports could be vital for the Chronicler's understanding of sacrifice.   The sacrificing done in 5:6 was not a cultic event performed in the temple.   The text is not specific about location, and the act

[71]Kurt Galling, *Die Bücher der Chronik, Esra, and Nehemia* (Göttingen: Vandenhoeck & Ruprecht, 1954), p. 93.

[72]Wilhelm Rudolph, *Chronikbüchen* (Tübingen: Verlag J. C. B. Mohr, 1949), p. 211.

[73]Raymond B. Dillard, *II Chronicles*, WBC (Waco, Texas: Word Publishing, 1987), pp. 5-6. The outline of the chiasm is presented on these pages. Dillard's proposal takes further that of Williamson who pointed out the inclusio of temple building in 2:1 and 8:16. These are Dillard's third and third from last major chiastic elements.

[74]For a discussion of such numbers see J. W. Wenham, "Large Numbers in the Old Testament," *TynB*, 18 (1967), 49. Wenham calculated that it would take twenty slaughterings per minute for ten hours per day for twelve days to kill 142,000 animals. He proposed that numbers often had zeroes attached to the end for effect. In this case he opted for dividing by ten to get 2,200 oxen and 12,000 sheep, but there is no particular reason not to divide by 100 or even 1000.

is presented as a rather casual affair.[75] In 7:4-5 the sacrifice is at the temple and suddenly the number of animals becomes important.

Second, why does the description of the glory cloud in 7:1-3 involve sacrifice? What separates this sacrificial event from the two discussed above? As mentioned earlier, the origin of the burnt offerings and sacrifices consumed in 7:1 is not explained by the text. Their sudden appearance is consistent with the observation that the writer of Chronicles stayed very close to the Deuteronomistic source when using it.[76] The author did not alter the source to make this insertion fit neatly in every way. This point underscores the importance of the insertion for the writer of Chronicles. Aside from the possibility that 7:1-3 helps complete a literary chiasm, these verses portray the first sacrificial act in Solomon's temple as one enacted by God personally. The dedication ritual in 7:4-5 is secondary. Solomon's consecration of the court, burnt offerings, and offerings of well-being in 7:7 are an afterthought. The full impact of this observation will have to wait for the discussion of the final sacrificial act in Solomon's temple (II Chronicles 36:17).

The other sacrificial events analyzed in this chapter will be from II Chronicles 29-36, material that is not paralleled in the Deuteronomistic History.[77] What has become apparent here is that in one of the few texts describing sacrifice that the author of Chronicles did take from the earlier history an insertion was made which altered the nature and understanding of the event.

---

[75]That these animals could not be counted while the 142,000 (or some factor thereof) could be in 7:4-5 would indicate that there was less concern for organization in the portrayal of this first event.

[76]McKenzie, *The Chronicler's Use*, p. 113.

[77]Ibid., p. 187. As noted in the introduction, the Chronicler ceased using the Deuteronomistic source at the beginning of chapter 29.

Hezekiah's Reform

II Chronicles 29:20-36

20 Hezekiah the king rose early and gathered the officials of the city, and he went up to the house of the Lord. 21 They brought seven bulls, seven rams, seven lambs, and seven male goats for a sin offering for the kingdom, for the sanctuary, and for Judah,[78] and he told the sons of Aaron, the priests, to make offerings upon the altar of the Lord. 22 They slaughtered the bull and the priests took the blood and they threw it on the altar, and they slaughtered the rams and threw the blood on the altar, and they slaughtered the lambs and threw the blood on the altar. 23 They brought the he-goats of the sin offering before the king and the assembly, and they laid their hands upon them. 24 The priests slaughtered them and they offered their blood on the altar to atone for all Israel, because the king said the burnt offering and the sin offering are for all Israel.

25 He stationed the Levites in the house of the Lord with cymbals, harps, and lyres by the commandment of David, Gad the seer of the king, and Nathan the prophet; for by the hand of the Lord was this commandment, by the hand of his prophet. 26 The Levites stood with the instruments of David and the priests with their trumpets. 27 Hezekiah commanded that burnt offerings be made for the altar, and at the same time as the beginning of the burnt offering was the time of the beginning of the song of the Lord, the trumpets, and upon the hands of[79] the instruments of David, king of Israel. 28 The whole assembly was worshiping, the singers were singing, and the trumpeters were playing, the whole of it,[80] until the end of the burnt offering. 29 At the end of the offering the king and all the ones present with him bowed down and worshiped. 30 Hezekiah the king, and the officials, commanded the Levites to praise the Lord in the words of David and Asaph the seer. And they praised to the point of joy and bowed down and worshiped. 31 Hezekiah answered and said, "Now you have consecrated your hands to the Lord. Draw near and bring sacrifices and thank offerings to the house of the Lord." And the assembly brought sacrifices and thank offerings, and all of a willing heart brought burnt offerings. 32 The number of the burnt offerings which

---

[78]LXX replaces "Judah" with "Israel."

[79]LXX replaces the awkward phrase "and upon the hands of" with the preposition *pros*, meaning "in addition to" or "with."

[80]LXX, Syriac, and Vulgate omit the phrase "the whole of it."

the assembly brought was seventy bulls, 100 rams, and 200 male lambs. For a burnt offering for the Lord were all of these. 33 And the sanctified ones were 600 bulls and 3000 sheep. 34 But the priests were few in number and were not able to skin all the burnt offerings; so their brothers, the Levites, helped them until the end of the work and until the priests had sanctified themselves, for the Levites were more upright in heart to sanctify themselves than the priests. 35 Also the burnt offerings were great with the fat of the offerings of well-being and drink offerings for the burnt offering. And the service of the house of the Lord was restored. 36 And Hezekiah and all of the people rejoiced for what God did for the people, for with suddenness was the matter accomplished.

The account of Hezekiah's purifying of the temple and reinstitution of the sacrificial cult is a stunning spectacle. Nowhere in the Deuteronomistic History, or up to this point in Chronicles, has there been so vivid a portrayal of a sacrificial event. No longer is there a simple recording of the act and its sponsor, with perhaps a few numbers delineating the size of the event. Suddenly, the pages of the Bible are filled with slaughtered beasts, blood flying onto the altar, skins ripped off, and fat burning. This event is not recorded in the Deuteronomistic History, so the Chronicler did not have this influence upon his narrative, and his strong interest in sacrificial ritual shows here.

The first half of II Chronicles 29 records Hezekiah's reopening of the temple. The lowly condition of Judah at the time is explained (vv. 7-8). The sacrificial cult had ceased to operate under the reign of Ahaz. To amend the situation the priests and the Levites went back into the temple, at the urging of Hezekiah, to cleanse and sanctify it, preparing the utensils and the altar for the great day ahead.

II Chronicles 29:20-36 has a rather complex structure. The first two major blocks, vv. 20-24 and vv. 25-30, appear to parallel one another; the priests bring offerings in the first section and the Levites in the second. A possible solution is to identify two hands at work in the narrative. Adam

Welch, who championed this position, labelled vv. 25-30 the original work of the Chronicler and vv. 21-24 an addition by a later redactor, anxious to give the priests their due.[81] David L. Petersen has developed this view further, while altering it significantly. Rather than an original version and a later addition, Petersen has identified two originally separate sources brought together by the author of Chronicles into a framework supported by Leviticus 1:4-9. Leviticus prescribes two steps to sacrifice of purification, a blood rite (II Chronicles 29:20-24) and an altar burning (II Chronicles 29:25-30).[82] The purpose of this structure was to empower the Levites.[83] Dillard has argued on the contrary, that the two events describe the same event from two different perspectives.[84]

The argument for the unity of the passage as the work of the Chronicler began with Wilhelm Rudolph, who argued that 29:27 makes it clear that the Levitical singing is simultaneous with the burnt offerings. After a description of the sacrificial event in vv. 20-24, the Chronicler wished to emphasize the role of the Levites in vv. 25-30. The passage is therefore best treated as a whole.[85] Williamson picked up this line of argument, asserting that "The Chronicler's particular interest in the Levites, evident throughout the entire chapter, is sufficient to explain why he brought their role into

---

[81]Adam C. Welch, *The Work of the Chronicler: Its Purpose and Date* (London: Oxford University Press, 1939), pp. 106-107.

[82]David L. Petersen, *Late Israelite Prophecy: Studies in Deutero-Prophetic Literature and in Chronicles* (Missoula, Montana: Scholar's Press, 1977), p. 83. Petersen made much of the "evolution of sacrificial practice" from one stage where the offerer (layperson) killed the animal to that in which the priest did the killing. This concern is misplaced here, as there were no laypersons offering the animals slaughtered in 29:24. The issue is of some note when the assembly begins bringing its offerings in 29:32.

[83]Ibid., p. 85.

[84]Dillard, *II Chronicles*, p. 235.

[85]Rudolph, *Chronikbüchen*, p. 293.

prominence in this way."[86]

Those arguing for an addition to the original text in vv. 21-24 have not made their case adequately. The narrative hardly seems complete with vv. 21-24 excised. The Chronicler's concern for numbers during the sacrifice by the whole assembly in vv. 31-36 would be unparalleled during the priestly sacrifice if vv. 25-30 stood alone. If the proper involvement of the priests had been the motive for adding to the text, a much simpler alteration than the addition of vv. 21-24 could certainly have accomplished this goal. The present text holds together as a powerful, dramatic account.

Jacob Milgrom has raised some additional issues related to the number of animals in 29:21-24 and the apparent change in the recipient of the sacrifice from v. 21 ("for the kingdom, the sanctuary, and for Judah") to v. 24 ("for all Israel"). Assuming that there were seven bulls, rams, lambs and he-goats each for the kingdom, the sanctuary, and Judah, Milgrom obtained a total of eighty-four animals (seven times four times three). In v. 24 the three-fold recipient of the sacrificial atonement has been changed simply to "all Israel." The total of eighty-four would still hold significance here in providing a perfect seven animals for each of the twelve tribes. Milgrom further proposed that Hezekiah's ambition to reunite the kingdom is revealed in this decision to make atonement for "all Israel."[87] The weakness of this attempt is that twenty-one of each type of animal could not be divided equally among the twelve tribes. Thus, each tribe would not have received an identical group.[88] A change in recipient may not need explaining if "all Israel" is

---

[86]Williamson, *1 and 2 Chronicles*, p. 358.

[87]Jacob Milgrom, "Hezekiah's Sacrifices at the Dedication Services of the Purified Temple," in *Biblical and Related Studies Presented to Samuel Iwry*, ed. Ann Kort and Scott Morschauser (Winona Lake, Indiana: Eisenbrauns, 1985), p. 160.

[88]Milgrom acknowledged this difficulty but dismissed its significance, claiming that the whole sacrifice was for all Israel. The dismissal of this problem may be too hasty, especially considering that a problem of division motivated the original re-figuring from twenty-eight animals to eighty-four.

understood as a summation of the original three-fold entity - the kingdom, the sanctuary, and Judah.[89]

The continuation of sacrifice by the people in vv. 31-36 completed the event. Just as in II Chronicles 7, a smaller ceremony involving the presence of the priests was followed by a massive sacrifice at which the whole assembly was present. Thus, Hezekiah became a new Solomon by re-establishing the temple. Ironically, what seems to be a positive move toward reform, and the desperate attempts at reform to follow, form an integral part of Judah's downward spiral toward the Exile, as portrayed by the Chronicler in these frantic, final chapters.

Hezekiah's Passover
II Chronicles 30:1-27

1 Hezekiah sent unto all Israel and Judah, and he also wrote letters unto Ephraim and Manasseh to come to the house of the Lord in Jerusalem, to celebrate a Passover for the Lord, the God of Israel. 2 For the king had taken counsel, with his officials and all the assembly in Jerusalem, to celebrate a Passover in the second month. 3 But they were not able to do it at this time because the priests had not sanctified themselves sufficiently, and the people had not gathered themselves in Jerusalem. 4 But the thing was right in the eyes of the king and all the assembly. 5 So they formulated a proclamation to send forth a call throughout all Israel, from Beer-sheba to Dan, to come to celebrate a Passover to the LORD, the God of Israel, in Jerusalem; for not many had done it as prescribed. 6 Messengers went forth with the letter from the hand of the king and his officials through all Israel, and[90] according to the command of the king saying, "Sons of Israel return unto the LORD, the God of Abraham, Isaac, and

---

[89]Searches for symbolism in the number of animals sacrificed in Chronicles will usually end up fruitless. The contention of this study is that the striking elements of the sacrificial events in Chronicles are the graphic nature of their portrayal and their immensity. It should also be noted that the Targum of II Chronicles changes 29:21 to read "for the kingdom and for the sanctuary and for the men of Judah." The addition of "men" cleared up some of the confusion in the Aramaic version.

[90]LXX and Vulgate delete the conjunction.

Israel, and he will turn unto the remnant of you having escaped from the hand of the kings[91] of Assyria. 7 You were not like your fathers and like your brothers who were faithless to the LORD, the God of their fathers; and he gave them for a desolation, as you see. 8 Now do not stiffen your neck like your fathers. Give a hand to the LORD and come to his sanctuary, which he sanctified forever; and serve the LORD your God, and the fierceness of his anger will turn from you. 9 For if you turn, your brothers and your children will receive compassion before their captors to return to this land; for gracious and compassionate is the LORD your God, and he will not turn his face from you if you turn unto him. 10 The couriers were passing from city to city in Ephraim and Manasseh unto Zebulon, but they were ridiculing them and mocking them. 11 But men from Asher and from Manasseh, and from Zebulon humbled themselves and came to Jerusalem. 12 Also, the hand of God was upon Judah giving them one heart to do the commandment of the king, and of the officials, by the word of the Lord.

13 Many people gathered in Jerusalem to celebrate the festival of Unleavened Bread in the second month, a very great assembly. 14 They rose up and removed the altars which were in Jerusalem, and all the incense altars they took and threw into the Brook Kidron. 15 They slaughtered the Passover lamb on the fourteenth of the second month. The priests and Levites were ashamed, so they sanctified themselves and brought burnt offerings to the house of the Lord. 16 They stood at their places, according to their custom, according to the law of Moses, the man of God. The priests threw the blood from the hand of the Levites. 17 For there were many in the assembly who had not sanctified themselves, so the Levites were slaughtering the Passover lambs for all who were not clean to sanctify them before the LORD. 18 For a multitude of the people, many from Ephraim and Manasseh, Issachar and Zebulon were not clean, so the Passover was not according to what is written. But Hezekiah prayed over them saying, "Good LORD will still atone 19 for everyone whose heart is set to seek God, the LORD, the God of their fathers, even if not according to the cleanness of the sanctuary." 20 The LORD heard Hezekiah and healed the people.

The children of Israel present in Jerusalem celebrated the feast of Unleavened Bread seven days with great joy; and the Levites and the priests praised the Lord day by day, with strong instruments to the Lord. 22 Hezekiah spoke to the heart of all the Levites, the ones showing good skill for the LORD. They ate[92] the festival meal seven

---

[91] Singular in LXX, Syriac, and Vulgate.

[92] LXX has "they completed."

days, sacrificing sacrifices of peace and giving thanks to the LORD, the God of their fathers. 23 The whole assembly agreed to do so seven days more, and they did so with joy for seven days.   24 So Hezekiah, king of Judah, gave the assembly 1000 bulls and 7000 sheep, and the officials gave the assembly 1000 bulls and 10,000 sheep; and the priests sanctified themselves[93] in large numbers. 25 The whole assembly of Judah rejoiced, including the priests and the Levites, the whole assembly coming from Israel, the aliens coming from the land of Israel, and the ones dwelling in Judah. 26 Great joy was in Jerusalem, for from the days of Solomon, son of David king of Israel, it had not[94] been like this in Jerusalem. 27 The priests and the Levites arose and blessed the people, and their voice was heard. Their prayer came to his holy dwelling place in the heavens.

A primary critical issue for this passage is the question of its historicity. The Passover of Hezekiah is entirely absent from the Deuteronomistic history. The prior history does record Josiah's Passover, however, which raises the speculation that the Chronicler merely copied the event back into Hezekiah's reign to make him more nearly Josiah's equal in reform.[95]   As with Hezekiah's reform, the description of the Passover is preoccupied with the details of the sacrificial act, putting the number of animals slaughtered in the thousands. Once again there is much attention to the issue of cleanness. The most striking and unique point of this narrative, however, is the exception made for the members of some northern tribes who partook of the Passover

---

[93]LXX has "and the holy things of the priests."

[94]LXX has "there was no feast."

[95]For an illustration of this very common position see Roland Devaux, *Ancient Israel: Its Life and Institutions*, trans. John McHugh (New York: McGraw Hill Book Co., Inc., 1961), p. 471. The statements in II Chronicles 35:18 and II Kings 23:22 that no Passover like Josiah's had been kept since the period before the monarchy are used as proof that there was no great Passover in Hezekiah's day. On the contrary, the Chronicler's inclusion of this statement indicates that he did not see it as a denial of Hezekiah's Passover. There were differences which made each of the two events unique enough to make such claims. These will be discussed further along in this section and in the interpretation of II Chronicles 35. In addition to such differences, the preliminary observation should be noted that the passage in II Kings 23: 21-23 is a bare mention that Josiah kept a Passover. If the Chronicler's account of Hezekiah's Passover might be a fabrication, then the description of Josiah's is just as likely so.

without being formally clean.[96]

Before interpreting this passage further, it will help to examine some of the background relating to Passover. Passover is first mentioned in the narrative of Exodus 12. Two separate sets of instructions appear in this chapter. The first set, 12:1-20, is a highly detailed, legalistic command which has characteristics consistent with the P material in the Pentateuch. This set of instructions places the date of Passover on the fourteenth of the first month, links it with the festival of Unleavened Bread, and requires an assembly of the people. Exodus 12: 21-23 gives a greatly abbreviated list of instructions. This is possibly an earlier account, part of the J material of the Pentateuch.[97] The focus is on Passover as a family celebration. It was not yet a pilgrimage feast linked to Unleavened Bread. Leviticus 23:4-8, from the Holiness Code, places Passover on the fourteenth of the first month followed by the seven day festival of Unleavened Bread. Both are classified as pilgrimage festivals.

Deuteronomy 16:1-8 presents a different picture of Passover. It requires a gathering in Jerusalem ("The place that the Lord your God shall choose as a dwelling place for his name"). Passover is to be in the month of *Abib*, but no day is given. Little detail is supplied about the sacrificial process. Emphasis is on the location of the event, which is consistent with

---

[96]This forms the basis of the most telling argument that Hezekiah's Passover is not a fabrication based on Josiah's. Why would the Chronicler have fashioned a narrative with that purpose and added a bizarre element which called Hezekiah's orthodoxy into question? See Dillard, *II Chronicles*, p. 240. Dillard reached the conclusion that it is more probable that the Deuteronomistic Historian omitted material about Hezekiah in order to elevate the status of Josiah.

[97]Judson R. Shaver, *Torah and the Chronicler's History Work: An Inquiry into the Chronicler's Reference to Laws, Festivals and Cultic Institutions in Relationship to Pentateuchal Legislation* (Atlanta: Scholars Press, 1989), p. 105. In this work Shaver presented a full developmental scheme for the celebrations of Passover and Unleavened Bread.

Deuteronomy's agenda of centralization.[98]

The stipulations for Passover and Unleavened Bread in Numbers 28:16-25 are very similar to those found in Leviticus 23.[99] One additional passage in Numbers is vital to the understanding of the Hezekiah account. In Numbers 9:6-11 Moses resolved the problem of an unclean group desiring to celebrate the Passover by allowing them to do so exactly one month later on the fourteenth day of the second month.

Which of these Passover traditions was Hezekiah following in the Chronicler's narrative? There has been a wide variance of opinion on this question. Haran argued that the whole of Hezekiah's reform movement reflects the tradition connected with the P material of the Torah.[100] DeVaux likewise concluded that the P tradition was the pattern for Hezekiah's Passover.[101] Gerhard von Rad, on the other hand, claimed that the tradition in Deuteronomy was the model for Hezekiah's Passover.[102] Shaver has aptly pointed out that this confusion is the result of a mixing of traditions in II Chronicles 30. The location of Hezekiah's Passover was Jerusalem, as stipulated by Deuteronomy. The timing of the celebration, delayed by one month, followed the ruling in Numbers 9. The performance of the ritual itself was most closely associated with the Yahwist material found

---

[98]Ibid., p. 106. Shaver pointed out that the vocabulary about Passover changes. In Exodus 21 the animal was "killed" (ש ח ט), but in Deuteronomy 16 it was to be "sacrificed" (ז ב ח). Shaver's book incorrectly identified this second root as ז ב ה.

[99]Ibid., p. 107. Shaver identified Numbers 28 as the latest layer of development in Passover and Unleavened Bread tradition found in the Torah.

[100]Menahem Haran, *Temples and Temple Services in Ancient Israel: An Inquiry into the Character of Cult Phenomena and the Historical Setting of the Priestly School* (Oxford: The Clarendon Press, 1978), p. 141. This position appears to be tied to the assumption that the Hezekiah Passover is entirely non-historical.

[101]DeVaux, *Ancient Israel*, p. 487.

[102]Gerhard von Rad, *Das Geschichtsbild des Chronistischen Werkes* (Stuttgart: Kohlhammer, 1930), p. 52-53.

in Exodus 12:21-32.[103] The disagreement has been the result of an assumption that the Chronicler was following only one tradition in describing Hezekiah's Passover.

If the Chronicler's account of Hezekiah's Passover is eclectic, not attempting to uphold any particular tradition, then what is the agenda of the passage? First, it was essential that all of Israel should take part in the celebration. In order to accomplish this, Hezekiah had to enact a one month delay. This moved the celebration to the next acceptable date and allowed time for the proper preparations to be made. Though certainly based on Numbers 9, this decision went an important step further. In Numbers, the Passover was carried out in the first month as called for, with only those who had been unclean waiting until the second month. In II Chronicles 30, the entire ceremony was delayed one month so that the northern tribes might participate along with everyone else.[104] The desire for unified participation also created the need to make use of the Deuteronomic tradition. An additional seven days were added to the feast (30:23), following the precedent of extension established by Solomon in II Chronicles 7:8-10.[105] The extra seven days provided a further opportunity for the massive sacrifices recorded in 30:24.[106]

---

[103]Shaver, *Torah*, pp. 110-112.

[104]See S. Talmon, "Calendar-Reckoning in Ephraim and Judah," *VT*, 8 (1958), 61. Talmon asserted that the reason for the delay was a concession to the Samarians, whose calendar was one month different from that of Judah. The Chronicler hid Hezekiah's deference by blaming the slovenly priests who were unprepared. Also, the return of Josiah to the Judean calendar, by observing Passover in the first month, is another justification for the claim of uniqueness in II Chronicles, without denying the historicity of Hezekiah's Passover (p. 63). See also Frederick L. Moriarty, "The Chronicler's Account of Hezekiah's Reign," *CBQ*, 27 (1965), 405.

[105]Williamson, *1 and 2 Chronicles*, PP. 368-369. Williamson observed the borrowed wording from Solomon's prayers that appears in Hezekiah's speech in II Chronicles 30:6-9.

[106]J. G. McConville, *Law and Theology in Deuteronomy* (Sheffield: JSOT Press, 1984), p. 117. McConville noted the blurring of the lines of distinction, such that the sacrifices associated with Unleavened Bread became connected with Passover and Unleavened Bread as a single entity.

The result of this conglomeration of traditions was a massive sacrificial ceremony in which all of Israel participated.[107] This was the priority of the Chronicler's portrayal. Even the usual preoccupation with ritual purity was abandoned in 30:18-20.[108] Yahweh accepted the offering despite the violation and "healed the people." Nevertheless, the result was only a stay of execution for Judah which, after this brief period of renewal, continued its inevitable downward slide.

Josiah's Reform
II Chronicles 34:1-7

1 Josiah was eight years old when he became king; and for thirty-one years he reigned in Jerusalem. 2 He did right in the eyes of the Lord, and he walked in the ways of David, his ancestor, and he did not turn aside to the right or to the left. 3 In the eighth year of his reign, while he was still a young man, he began to seek the God of David his ancestor. In the twelfth year he began to purify Judah and Jerusalem from the high places, the Asherim, the images, and the pillars. 4 They pulled down the altars of Baal in his presence, and the incense altars which were above them he cut down. He broke into pieces the Asherim, the images, and the pillars and he crushed them into dust, and he threw it upon the surfaces of the graves of the ones sacrificing to them. 5 He burned the bones of the priests upon their altars, and he purified Judah and Jerusalem. 6 In the cities of Manasseh, Ephraim, Simeon, Naphtali, and in their places[109] all

---

[107]Johann Maier, *The Temple Scroll: An Introduction, Translation and Commentary* (Sheffield: JSOT Press, 1985), p. 78. Maier found that the Passover regulations in the Temple Scroll of Qumran were much more strict than those found in the Torah. A tightly defined ceremony may then have been a relatively late development, while a patchwork of traditions was still acceptable in the Chronicler's era.

[108]The Targum of Chronicles reports that a second Passover was repeated strictly according to the law to make up for the questionable first performance.

[109]The text of MT, ם ה י ת ב ר ה ב , is considered corrupt here, possibly as a result of a mistake in the Leningrad Codex. The *qere*, ם ה ׳ ת ב ר ה ב (with their swords), is readable but makes little sense. A simple metathesis of ר and ח produces a form which matches the "in their streets" of LXX. Another option is to read with II Kings 23:19 "in their shrines." For a more complete discussion of this textual problem see Dillard, *II Chronicles*, p. 275.

around, 7 he broke down the altars. He crushed the Asherim and the images into dust. He cut down all the incense altars in all the land of Israel, and he returned to Jerusalem.

Following the wickedness of Manasseh and Amon, Josiah took the throne, providing one last pause in the demise of Judah. Again, the efforts at reform involved a great emphasis on sacrifice. At first glance, II Chronicles 34:1-7 may appear to have little or nothing to do with sacrifice, but this conclusion might be changed drastically by a careful reading of v. 5.

Unlike other examples of the Chronicler's work examined in this study, such as the expanded Passover accounts, II Chronicles 34:3-7 is a greatly abbreviated version of an episode appearing in the Deuteronomistic History (II Kings 23:1-20).[110] Though II Chronicles 34:5 is rather vague, its predecessor in II Kings 23:20 explicitly states that in the towns of Samaria Josiah "Sacrificed all the priests of the high places which were there upon the altars and he burned the bones of men upon them." Previously at Bethel, according to II Kings 23:16, Josiah had the bones removed from nearby tombs and burned on the altar. The Chronicler was much more subtle in his report of this act.[111] He merely stated that Josiah burned the bones of the priests[112] upon the altars. Were these the bones of exhumed corpses as in II Kings 23:16, or the bones of sacrificed priests as in II Kings 23:20. The burning of either on the altars might be interpreted as an act of sacrifice. It is easiest to assume that the Chronicler was lumping together the two acts

---

[110]For some speculations as to why certain elements of the Kings account were not included here, see Dillard, *II Chronicles*, p. 278.

[111]Would a pious Jew living in the Chronicler's era have been troubled by an act of human sacrifice, regardless of its motivation? Could this be a possible reason for the veiled description?

[112]The Targum's כ ו מ ר י א could be translated as "priests," but it may be rendered "sacrificers" as by R. LeDeaut and J. Robert. This interpretation would provide one more allusion to the true meaning of the act. See R. LeDeaut and J. Robert, *Targum des Chroniques, Tome I: Introduction and Traduction* (Rome: Biblical Institute Press, 1971), p. 172.

recorded in II Kings 23.[113] Any conclusion on this point is uncertain.

The key to this event in Chronicles is the change in the explanation of Josiah's motivation from that reported in Kings. In II Kings 23:16, the bones of the corpses were burned on the altar in order to defile it. No specific motivation is given for the sacrifice of the priests in II Kings 23:20. According to the Chronicler Josiah's burning of the priests on the altars had precisely the opposite effect. Rather than defiling, II Chronicles 34:5 declares that this " . . . purified Judah and Jerusalem." Therefore, despite its subtlety, the Chronicler's account of Josiah's reform portrays an event which functioned as an act of sacrifice. This purification cleared the way for the reforming of temple worship recorded in the remainder of chapter 35. The Chronicler's reordering of events, by placing the finding of the book of the law after Josiah's reforms, further highlights his personal piety as the motivation for reform.[114] For his actions Josiah received a mixed blessing (II Chronicles 34:28). Judah would still suffer disaster, but not in Josiah's lifetime. Once again, Judah's demise was only delayed, not averted, by an act of sacrifice.

---

[113]Another difference in the Kings and Chronicles accounts occurs in the chronological markers used in the latter. While II Kings 22:3 reports that Josiah began his reforms in the eighteenth year of his reign, the twenty-sixth year of his life, II Chronicles 34:3 places the beginning in the twelfth year of his kingship. See Mordechai Cogan, "The Chronicler's Use of Chronology as Illuminated by Neo-Assyrian Royal Inscriptions," in *Empirical Models for Biblical Criticism*, ed. Jeffrey H. Tigay (Philadelphia: University of Pennsylvania Press, 1985), pp. 200-205. Based on a comparison of the successive editions of Esarhaddon's "Babylonian Inscription," Cogan demonstrated a practice of dating the beginning of all of a king's activities back to his accession year. This practice was designed to highlight the king's concern for all the affairs of the nation from the beginning of his reign. In the case of Josiah the purpose was "...to show the earliness and self motivation of the king's piety" (p. 205). Thus, in Chronicles the reforms were begun when Josiah was twenty, the youngest age at which he could act on his own.

[114]Dillard, *II Chronicles*, p. 277. The Chronicler may have reversed the order of events so that the sacrificial cleansing of Judah and Jerusalem would precede the reform of temple worship, a better sequence from his perspective.

Josiah's Passover:

II Chronicles 35:1-19

1 Josiah celebrated a Passover in Jerusalem for the Lord, and they slaughtered the Passover lamb on the fourteenth day of the first month. 2 He established the priests in their places, and he encouraged them for the service of the LORD. 3 He said to the Levites, the ones teaching all Israel, the holy ones of the LORD, "Put the holy ark in the house which Solomon, the son of David King of Israel, built. No longer are you to bear it upon your shoulder. Now serve the Lord your God and his people Israel. 4 Prepare yourselves for the house of your fathers according to your divisions, according to[115] the writing of David King of Israel and the writing of Solomon his son. 5 Stand in the sanctuary according to the groups of the house of the fathers, for your kindred, the children of the people; with a portion of a house of a father assigned to each of the Levites. 6 Kill the Passover lamb, sanctify yourselves, and prepare for your kindred to do so, according to the word of the Lord by the hand of Moses.

Josiah gave to the children of the people sheep and kids from the flocks for the Passover offerings for all present, to the number of 30,000 sheep and 3,000 bulls. These were from the possession of the king. 8 His officials gave for a free-will offering to the people, the priests, and the Levites. Hilkiah, Zechariah, and Jehiel, officers of the house of God, gave to the priests 2600 lambs for the Passover offerings and 300 bulls. 9 Cananiah, Shemaiah, Nethanel, his brothers, and Hashabiah, Jeiel, and Jozabad, the chiefs of the Levites, gave to the Levites 5,000 Passover offerings and 500 bulls. 10 The service was prepared, and the priests stood upon their place and the Levites in their divisions, according to the command of the king. 11 They slaughtered the Passover lamb, and the priests threw[116] from their hand, and the Levites were skinning. 12 They set aside the burnt offerings to give them to the groups of the house of the fathers, to the children of the people, to offer to the Lord as written in the book of Moses. Likewise they did with the bulls. 13 They roasted the Passover lamb in the fire according to the rule, and they boiled the sacrifices in the pots, in the cauldrons, and in the pans, and they gave them quickly to all the children of the people. 14 Afterward, they prepared for themselves and the priests, because the priests, the sons of Aaron, were offering the burnt offerings and the fat portions until night. The

---

[115]MT has "in the writing." LXX, Syriac, and Vulgate all contain "according to."

[116]LXX, Targum, and Vulgate add "the blood."

Levites offered for themselves, for the priests, and for the sons of Aaron. 15 The singers, the sons of Asaph, were upon their place according to the commandment of David, Asaph, Hemam, and Jedathun, the seer of the king, and the gatekeepers were keeping the gates. They did not leave their place of service because their brothers, the Levites, offered for them. 16 All the service of the LORD was prepared that day for celebrating the Passover and offering the burnt offerings on the altar of the LORD, according to the command of King Josiah. 17 The children of Israel, the ones present, celebrated the Passover at that time and the feast of Unleavened Bread for seven days. 18 A Passover like it had not been kept in Israel since the days of Samuel the prophet. All the kings of Israel did not conduct anything like the Passover which Josiah clebrated, along with the priests, the Levites, and all of Judah and Israel, the ones present, and the inhabitants of Jerusalem. 19 In the eighteenth year of the reign of Josiah this Passover was celebrated.

With the beginning of chapter 35 the parallel account in I Esdras offers a fascinating point of comparison for the Chronicler's narrative. If I Esdras is an intentional work using Chronicles, Ezra, and Nehemiah as sources,[117] why would the author have begun with Josiah's Passover? How do the differences in I Esdras 1:1-24[118] and II Chronicles 35:1-19 highlight the purposes of the two versions of this story?

Josiah's Passover in II Chronicles 35 is much longer and more detailed than the few sparse verse found in II Kings 23:21-23. First and foremost, what is present in the Chronicler's account is a massive sacrificial event described in graphic detail. 41,600 beasts were slaughtered, skinned, and burned. Again, the unrealistic numbers stress the urgency and importance of the event in hyperbolic fashion. The question arises, as with Hezekiah's Passover, as to which of Israel's traditions of Passover is expressed in this observance.

---

[117]This is the position of Tamara Eskenazi, "The Chronicler and the Composition of I Esdras," *CBQ*, 48 (1986), 39. For background discussion of the problem of I Esdras, see chapter one of this study.

[118]I Esdras 1:23-24 is not found in II Chronicles 35. These two verses were inserted between the accounts of Josiah's Passover and his death. They appear to belong more with the first unit.

DeVaux argued that the Deuteronomic tradition held sway, pointing to the emphasis of centralization of the ceremony in Jerusalem.[119] Shaver has countered again that certain elements of the P legislation indicate a mixing of traditions to create a rather unique Passover ceremony.[120] Apparently, the concern of the Chronicler was not to follow any particular set of legal stipulations. Rather, he has once again portrayed a massive sacrifice with all of Israel as its participants. Passover was intended to be a memorial to what occurred in Egypt hundreds of years before; but, given the magnificent frenzy of the pictures the Chronicler produced in the final few chapters, one must wonder whether these Passovers had more to do with the future than with the past.

The account in I Esdras 1:1-22 is nearly identical to that in II Chronicles 35:1-19. The one striking difference is the additional statement in I Esdras 1:10 that the priests and Levites stood in their places with the unleavened bread. In II Chronicles 35:10, the corresponding verse, there is no mention of unleavened bread. Thus, the compiler of I Esdras has gone even further in the type of blending of traditions discussed above.

Eskenazi has proposed that I Esdras is a "distinct composition."[121] The purpose of the author in composing a narrative made up essentially of II Chronicles 35-36, all of Ezra, and Nehemiah 8 was to " . . . bring the material from Ezra-Nehemiah into conformity with the ideology and style of the book of Chronicles."[122] Can this proposal assist in understanding the structure and purpose of this part of Chronicles? If this was the intent of the author of I Esdras, whom Eskenazi associates very closely with the Chronicler, then

---

[119]DeVaux, *Ancient Israel*, p. 487.

[120]Shaver, *Torah*, pp. 115-116. The date of Passover mentioned explicitly in II Chronicles 35:1 has the calendar in Leviticus 23:5-8 as its source. The roasting of the animal in II Chronicles 35:13 is associated with Exodus 12.

[121]Eskenazi, "The Chronicler...," 39.

[122]Ibid., 40.

evidently this author felt that these final two chapters came close to epitomizing all of Chronicles. To address this point, it will be necessary to examine a few elements of Eskenazi's argument. She has outlined four critical elements of the Chronicler's ideology: (1) The centrality of David, (2) the concept of all-Israel, (3) retribution and prophecy, and (4) temple and cult.[123] First, David is mentioned three times in II Chronicles 35:1-19. He was the author of this Passover (v.4). Second, the Passover was celebrated by all of Israel together (vv. 17-18). Third, the short-lived blessings Josiah received as a result of his reforms, and his death as a result of disobedience are an illustration of immediate retribution. Eskenazi did observe that the additions in I Esdras 1:21-22 and 1:28 highlight the theme of retribution and the role of the prophet Jeremiah.[124] Finally, the whole of I Esdras is bracketed by two great temple events, with Josiah's Passover forming the front end. Thus, with only minor, perhaps unnecessary additions, the Chronicler's record of Josiah's life was able to serve as a microcosm for the whole of Chronicles.

In II Chronicles 34:28 Josiah received a promise and a dire warning from the Lord. Judah would be spared during his lifetime, but utter destruction was coming eventually. The purpose of the original Passover was to keep the plague of the death of the firstborn away from the houses of the Hebrews in Egypt. As mentioned earlier, the fixation upon Passover in the final chapters of II Chronicles can hardly be a mere attempt to memorialize the past. The final plague was once again lurking on the horizon. The effectiveness of these attempts to prevent the death of the firstborn of Israel will be examined in the next section.

---

[123]Ibid., 41-45.

[124]Ibid., pp. 52-53.

The Destruction of Judah

II Chronicles 36:15-21

15 The Lord, the God of their fathers, sent unto them by the hand of his messengers, sending repeatedly, for he had compassion upon his people and upon his dwelling. 16 But they mocked the messengers of God, despised his words, and scoffed at his prophets, until the anger of the LORD rose up against his people, and there was no healing. 17 So he brought up against them the King of the Chaldeans, and he killed by the sword the young people of Israel in the house of their sanctuary. He had no mercy on young man or virgin, old or feeble. All of them he gave into his hand. 18 All the vessels of the house of God, large and small, and the treasures of the house of the Lord and the treasures of the king and his officials he brought to Babylon. 19 They burned the house of God and they broke down the wall of Jerusalem. All its palaces they burned with fire, and all its precious vessels were included in the destruction. 20 He took into exile in Babylon the ones escaping from the sword, and they became servants to him and his sons until the establishment of the kingdom of Persia; 21 to fulfill the word of the Lord in the mouth of Jeremiah, until the land made up its sabbaths. All the days of desolation the land kept sabbath, to fulfill seventy years.

The movement of the Chronicler's narrative toward Judah's annihilation is swift and sure. The fifty-seven verses of II Kings describing the period from Jehoahaz to the Exile are compressed into a brief twenty-one verse account in II Chronicles 35, as if the death of Josiah cut the final thread by which Judah clung for its life, creating a free-fall into destruction.

The destruction was introduced by one final explanation of its cause in vv. 15-16. The people had not heeded the message of God. This leads to the most striking element of the final narrative. In v. 17, "He [the Lord, from v. 16] brought up against them the King of the Chaldeans. The verb in this clause is ויעל , the *hiphil* imperfect of עלה with a ו consecutive. The second and third clauses both contain a *qal* third masculine singular verb form with no explicit subject. The fourth and final clause of the verse has God as its pronominal subject without any doubt.[125] Are the subjects of בְּ יְ הָ רְ נ (and he killed) and חָ מַ ל (he had mercy) intended to be God or the king of the Chaldeans?[126] Most versions of the Bible in English unfortunately insert a relative pronoun in front of "killed," making it clear that the King of the Chaldeans is the subject. Paul R. Rabbe has correctly pointed out that the temptation when ambiguity is encountered is to choose one alternative and argue vehemently for it. Instead Rabbe says, "My contention is that sometimes, maybe more often than we think, a word, phrase, or sentence could be understood in two (or more) ways because both were intended. It is deliberately ambiguous."[127] Rather than falling to the common temptation, this interpretation will assume that both God and the king of the chaldeans were intended as subjects of the verbs in the second and third clauses of 36:17.

The possible confusion created by the ambiguity in v. 17 should not obscure the powerful message of this verse. The parallel account in II Kings 25 gives more detail about the siege and destruction of the city, but contains no reference to the killing of the young people in the temple. The parallel narrative in I Esdras 1:53 reads,"These slew their young men with the sword around their holy temple." The ambiguity of subject is removed by the insertion of a plural demonstrative, and the subtle insertion of περικυλω dramatically changes the location of the killing. All of this serves to intensify the impact of the Chronicler's portrayal. This action may be interpreted as a sacrificial event. When young (innocent) persons are slaughtered in the

---

[125]That the first and last clauses of v. 17 have third masculine singular pronouns as subjects for which God, in v. 16, is clearly the antecedent makes reading the King of the Chaldeans as the subject of the middle two clauses more difficult.

[126]Dillard, *II Chronicles*, p. 301. Dillard mentioned the possibility that God could be read as the subject of the second and third clause, but called this conclusion "improbable."

[127]Paul R. Rabbe, "Deliberate Ambiguity in the Psalter," *JBL*, 110 (1991), 213. See Rabbe's discussion of ambiguity created by an "unspecified subject or object" of a verb (p. 219).

sanctuary, it is difficult to ignore the potential sacrificial elements of such an act.[128]

The void of detail found in 36:17 might be filled if the previous two events in the temple are etched in the reader's mind. Could the graphic accounts of the Passovers of Hezekiah and Josiah supply the bloody details for this slaughter? With a number of young persons being killed by the sword in the temple, it is easy enough to imagine blood flying onto the altar. When the temple was burned in 36:19, the reader might possibly picture the bodies of these dead young people being roasted like the 41,600 beasts at Josiah's Passover.

Williamson has emphasized the literary techniques used by the Chronicler to heighten the effect of his message in the final chapter. By shortening the account of each king, removing elements such as the death notices, emphasis was placed on matters involving the temple. Thus, the pace toward exile was accelerated, increasing the focus on the climactic conclusion.[129] These observations concerning chapter 36 provide even greater reason for seeing v. 17 as the goal to which the final chapters, if not the whole of Chronicles, has been leading.

The Chronicler's Theology of Sacrifice

The foregoing analysis of some of the literary elements of the great sacrificial events in Chronicles should provide some clues for interpreting the chronicler's overall understanding of sacrifice. If the discussion thus far has been essentially correct, then the key verse for understanding sacrifice in Chronicles is II Chronicles 36:17. If this event left the temple, or temple site,

---

[128]Was the vagueness of the Chronicler's report due to a distaste for the idea of human sacrifice? Recall that a similar subtlety was present in II Chronicles 34:5 in the story of the burning of the bones of the priests on the altars of the high places.

[129]Williamson, *1 and 2 Chronicles*, p. 412.

prepared for the Restoration, then its purpose was purification. The sacrifice of the Hebrew young people by God, and to God, is followed shortly at the end of the chapter by the decree of Cyrus. This is a most puzzling passage, especially in the abruptness of the ending it provides for Chronicles, indeed, even for the whole of the Hebrew canon.[130] This decree is certainly more than a Persian legal document. It is a rallying cry to support the new temple. How has the history of the fall of Judah, as recorded in II Chronicles, prepared the way for such a call?

In the final chapters of II Chronicles, there is a growing concern for temple activity. Chapters 29-36 portray two great reform movements and two massive, centralized festivals. Such intense activity in and around the temple is unprecedented in the Deuteronomistic History and in earlier portions of Chronicles. Even Solomon's dedication of the temple, though vital for understanding the end of Chronicles, lacks much of the vivid detail present in the events of the last eight chapters. Either the Chronicler or his major source for these chapters, or both, understood sacrifice as the determinative element in Judah's fate as a nation.[131]

II Chronicles 29-36, therefore, performed two primary tasks. It explained the horrifying fate of Judah in the recent past, and it provided a program for the future which could prevent a recurrence of such devastation. The perilous descent of Judah was surely underway with the wicked reign of Hezekiah's father, Ahaz. The end of II Chronicles 28 contains some foreboding elements, including the reports that Ahaz offered sacrifices to the gods of Damascus and Aram (v. 23), and that he was not buried in the tombs

---

[130]This ending is, of course, part of the great debate over the unity of Chronicles and Ezra, as outlined in the first chapter of this study. For a more constructive interpretation of these final verses, see Eskenazi, "The Chronicler . . . ," p. 57. Eskenazi has offered an intriguing alternative translation for the final word of the Hebrew canon, ל ע ׳ ו . If this form may be translated "let him sacrifice" as well as "let him go up," then the ending of Chronicles becomes, to an even greater extent, a polemic for the legitimacy of the second temple cult.

[131]It is in these final chapters, where the Chronicler parted most dramatically from the Deuteronomistic History, that his perspective should be most evident.

of Israel's kings (v. 27). These two verses contain alterations of and additions to the Deuteronomistic History. The massive reform movements of Hezekiah and Josiah were fleeting efforts to forestall the demise of Judah. Though the elements of the reforms contained important directives to the post-Exilic community, which will be discussed below, they were ultimately futile attempts which did not even maintain their momentum through the lifetimes of their sponsoring kings. Between the reforms of Hezekiah and Josiah were the reigns of two evil kings, Manasseh and Amon, who dragged Judah further toward destruction. Josiah's reform is punctuated by a rapid succession of kings in II Chronicles 36, leading up to the Babylonian invasion.

The decline of the Davidic line, with its occasional, brief upturns, was paralleled by the condition of the cult. The message of the Chronicler is that when sincere sacrifice was offered Judah's fortunes were good, but this had no lasting effect. The downward inertia could not be halted. The history of Solomon's temple ended as it had begun. In II Chronicles 7:1-3 the Chronicler inserted a report of fire pouring down from heaven to consume burnt offerings. A sacrifice performed by God enacted the inaugural purification of the temple. In II Chronicles 36:17, the ultimate sacrifice of Israel's young people was carried out by God through the agency of the Babylonian army. The temple was destroyed and, at the same time, purified for what was to come after the Exile.

To the post-Exilic community this was all more than mere historical data. The Chronicler offered vital instruction to those worshiping in the new Temple. In the words of Jacob M. Myers, "The history of the pre-Exilic nation is related as a warning to the post-Exilic community to remain both cultically and morally faithful, so as to avoid the fate that overtook the fathers."[132] The Chronicler urgently desired to connect the second temple

---

[132]Jacob M. Myers, "The Kerygma of the Chronicler," *Interp*, 20 (1966), 264-265. See also Richard Elliott Friedman, *The Exile and Biblical Narrative: The Formation of the Deuteronomistic and Priestly Works* (Chico, California: Scholar's Press, 1981), pp. 124-125. Friedman argued that the Priestly redactor of the Torah, who would have been active in the

cult with the reforms of the past. Wilson Chang has observed that the telescoping of the reigns of Judah's last kings from Jehoiakim to the Exile served to focus attention on the "...continuity of Israel's sacral institutions in the pre- and post-Exilic periods."[133] The ultimate price had been paid in order to purify the temple of Solomon. Faithfulness would be required in order to maintain that condition. Proper sacrifice was necessary to assure the survival of restored Israel.[134] Again in Myers words, "The Chronicler was convinced that the paramount way of salvation for the Jews in the post-Exilic age was by the maintenance of proper cultic observances."[135] This kind of emphasis seems most consistent with the position that Chronicles was compiled in the early days of second temple worship, in the late sixth century.

While the focus here has been on the importance of continuity with pre-Exilic Israel, the analysis of Ezra and Nehemiah to follow will show that a certain degree of discontinuity was also vital to the early polemic of the second temple.

---

same era as the Chronicler, altered its perspective to place more emphasis on human control of events. This shift may be paralleled in the Chronicler's message contained in the accounts of the great reform movements.

[133]Wilson Ilsan Chang, "The *Tendenz* of the Chronicler," (Ph.D. dissertation, Hartford Theological Seminary, 1973), p. 227. See also Williamson, *1 and 2 Chronicles*, p. 28. Williamson asserted that Chronicles actually reveals many of the practices of post-Exilic Israel. This points to the Chronicler's understanding that the temple cult was a powerful symbol of continuity with the pre-Exilic kingdom.

[134]Myers, "The Kerygma . . .," p. 267.

[135]Ibid., 269.

Chapter 3

SACRIFICIAL EVENTS IN EZRA AND NEHEMIAH

This chapter will take the same approach to the Ezra and Nehemiah passages as the last chapter did to those in Chronicles. A better understanding of the intention of Ezra and Nehemiah may be gained by looking at what took place between the end of Chronicles and the beginning of Ezra, in order to set some context.

The Temple and Sacrificial Cult
during the Exile

Exactly what happened to the temple in 586 B.C.E.? What forms of worship may have been carried on at the temple site during the Exile?[136] What was the nature of religious practice among the exiles in Babylon? The paucity of evidence makes these questions difficult to answer, but some glimpse may be gained by examining a few related texts in the Hebrew Bible.

II Chronicles 36:18-19 and II Kings 25:9-17 report that the temple was emptied of its treasures and burned by the Babylonians. Both accounts specifically mention the breaking down of the walls of Jerusalem, but they do

---

[136]See Bustanay Oded, "Judah and the Exile," in *Israelite and Judean History*, ed. John H. Hayes and J. Maxwell Miller (Philadelphia: Westminster Press, 1977), p. 478. The exact nature of the community which remained in Palestine has been debated. The old view that the land suffered severe destruction and that only a small population remained, has been called into question by arguments that the country was still largely intact and that most of the people remained.

not indicate that the temple was torn down. It may be reasonable to assume that a large part of the stone structure was left standing. On this point, D. Winton Thomas has argued that the walls of the temple remained, and that worship was continued within the burned-out shell of the structure.[137] On the other hand, D. R. Jones contended that sacrifice was halted at the temple after the destruction. Jones relied heavily upon the reports of Chronicles and Ezra to establish his position. The failure of the book of Ezra to mention specifically any kind of sacrificial worship would suggest that it did not happen.[138] While Jones used an unconvincing argument from silence, perhaps intentional silence, it is also true that the evidence from Chronicles and Ezra is insufficient to prove the position of Thomas.[139]

A more complete picture, however, may be gained from the

---

[137]D. Winton Thomas, "The Sixth Century B.C.: A Creative Epoch in the History of Israel," *JSS*, 6 (1961), 43. See also Morton Smith, *Palestinian Parties and Politics that Shaped the Old Testament* (London: SCM Press, 1987), p. 69.

[138]D. R. Jones, "The Cessation of Sacrifice after the Destruction of the Temple in 586 B.C.," *JTS*, 14 (1963), 13-17. Jones cited evidence from Trito-Isaiah and Psalm 51 that sacrifice was abandoned at the temple site and replaced by prayer and fasting. His position relies heavily on argument from silence and may be grounded in a misconception of sacrifice. His contention that the essence of sacrifice is "costing personal surrender to God," and that "sacrificial rites may be the liturgical expression of this or they may not" (pp. 30-31), is an oversimplification.

[139]Opinions vary widely as to the living conditions in Exilic-Palestine and the extent of the population. See Edwin M. Yamauchi, "The Archaeological Background of Ezra," *BSac*, 137 (1980), 196-197. Yamauchi reports estimates anywhere from 20,000 to 235,000. Any population estimate is necessarily based on either scant archaeological evidence or face value acceptance of biblical numbers. See Charles C. Torrey, *Ezra Studies* (New York: Ktav Publishing, 1970), p. 290. Torrey accepted the Jeremiah figure of 4600 deportees, leaving most of the population still in Palestine. See also Peter R. Ackroyd, *Exile and Restoration*, OTL (Philadelphia: Westminster Press, 1968), pp. 20-25 and Enno Janssen, *Juda in der Exilsheit: Ein Beitrag sur Frage der Entstehung des Judentums* (Göttingen: Vanderhoeck & Ruprecht, 1956), pp. 94-104. Ackroyd and Janssen contended that the destruction of the land was not extensive, and that civilization continued in Palestine. See William F. Albright, *The Archaeology of Palestine* (Baltimore: Penguin Books, 1949), pp. 130-142. Albright, on the other hand, argued that the destruction was thorough and that there was no sedentary population in Palestine throughout the middle of the sixth century. See also Charles E. Carter, "The Province of Yehud in the Persian Period: A Textual, Artifactual, and Geographic Approach," (Unpublished paper delivered at the Society of Biblical Literature, November, 1991). Carter's more recent population estimates are extremely low, placing the numbers for restored Judah in the fourth and fifth centuries between 10,000 and 20,000.

consideration of Haggai 2:10-14 and Jeremiah 41:4-5. Haggai 2:10-14 is the report of a prophetic event during the rebuilding of the temple. Haggai 2:15 indicates that the offerings which had been and were being brought were unclean. The temple and the altar had not been purified. That sacrifices were being conducted there before the completion and formal establishment of the second temple cult might indicate that they had never stopped.[140]

Jeremiah 41:4-5 offers even more direct indications that sacrifice was not discontinued at the site of the temple. These verses report that on the day after Gedaliah's death men from the north came to perform sacrifices at the temple. In the midst of the Exilic period sacrifices were being brought to the temple in Jerusalem.[141]

Williamson's recent argument that penitential liturgies or laments were being performed at the Exilic temple site does not preclude sacrifice.[142] Williamson located these liturgies buried within the biblical text at places like Nehemiah 9:5-37, Isaiah 63:7-64:11, and Zechariah 7:1-7, 8:18-23. He has also contended that the presence of these liturgies, especially in Zechariah, shows that their use continued in the second temple.[143] That these passages must be "excavated," in Williamson's terms, while references to sacrifice are

---

[140]The picture presented in Haggai creates a problem for the position that a large part of the temple structure still remained. Was there not a single stone remaining on top of another? Was even the foundation gone? The statement in Haggai 1:4 uses the root חרב to describe the old temple. See F. I. Anderson, "Who Built the Second Temple," *Australian Biblical Review*, 6 (1958), 1-35. Anderson argued effectively that though this term can imply thorough destruction it can just as easily mean neglect or desertion. See also R. J. Coggins, *Samaritans and Jews: The Origins of Samaritanism Reconsidered* (Atlanta: John Knox Press, 1975), p. 47. Coggins has provided more recent confirmation of Anderson's assessment.

[141]Oded, "Judah . . . ," p. 478. See also Nige Allan, "The Identity of the Jerusalem Priesthood During the Exile," *HJ*, 23 (1982), 262-266. Allan argued that both Jeremiah 41 and Ezekiel indicate regular worship at the temple site during the Exile. The conflict in Ezekiel 44 was due to the establishment of rural Levites as Jerusalem priests during the Exile.

[142]H. G. M. Williamson, "Laments at the Second Temple," *BRev*, 6 (1990), 16.

[143]H. G. M. Williamson, "Isaiah 63:7-64:11: Exilic Lament or Post-Exilic Protest," *ZAW*, 102 (1990), 58.

readily apparent may indicate which was the most vital form of worship. The use of these laments in the second temple, certainly side-by-side with sacrifice, provides further indication that they may have been used together during the Exile.[144] The probability that sacrifice did take place on the temple site during the Exile demands a reexamination of the passages in Ezra which have been used traditionally to argue that such sacrifices did not take place.

The religious practices of the returned exiles may be an even more difficult subject about which to form firm conclusions. Certainly, their religion had to take on alternative forms once they were in another country, without the temple to serve as a worship center. According to Werner Schmidt, it was their existence in a foreign, impure land which guided the exiles in their worship. The lament was a necessary form of worship under such conditions. Prayer services and Sabbath observance did not require the temple and, therefore, became prominent.[145] Circumcision, which was uncommon in Mesopotamia, took on increasing importance as a sign of separation from their Babylonian captors.[146]

The extent to which synagogue worship developed in Babylon during the Exile is debatable. Arvid S. Kapelrud took the position that Sabbath evolved in Babylon from a "tabu-day" to a day of worship. It became a gathering time for the exiled community to conduct services of prayer and public reading. Kapelrud did not provide a thorough explanation of the extent of this development during the Exile.[147] If synagogue worship had evolved into any formal pattern at that time, then it did so to meet the needs

---

[144]See Janssen, *Juda*, p. 101. According to Janssen the book of Lamentations provides evidence that priests were active in Jerusalem during the Exile.

[145]Werner H. Schmidt, *The Faith of the Old Testament* (Philadelphia: Westminster Press, 1983), p. 252.

[146]Ibid., p. 254.

[147]Arvid S. Kapelrud, *Israel from the Earliest Times to the Birth of Christ* (Oxford: Basil Blackwell, 1966), p. 107.

54

of a specific situation. It is difficult to believe that it would have been carried on in the same fashion after the return and the building of the second temple. On the other hand, as the sacrificial cult became highly centralized in the Jerusalem temple, both in pre-Exilic reforms and during the Restoration,it is easy to see why small groups in Palestine would have developed localized forms of worship. On this basis, E. Hammerschaimb contended that synagogue worship began in pre-Exilic Israel.[148]

Daniel K. Smith has outlined four basic survival mechanisms which tend to develop among peoples who are displaced captives of another culture. Only one of these is explicitly religious. Smith's fourth mechanism is "The creation or elaboration of patterns of ritual practice that emphasize ritual weapons or ritual resistance against foreign influence, often expressed in concerns over purity and pollution from foreign elements."[149] Smith identified this force as the motivation behind the P material of the Pentateuch.[150] The trauma of the Exile accounted for the final form of P, highlighted by an intense concern for separation. Smith explained this concern as an effort to maintain boundaries between a captive people and its captors. The emphasis on separation, and a resulting sense of holiness, served as a mechanism of survival for a minority people.[151] The exiles who strived to separate themselves were a minority, not only with respect to their Babylonian captors, but also with respect to other Israelites who were assimilating into the Babylonian culture. Such a heightened concern for purity and separation would seem to require the imminent threat of assimilation.

---

[148]E. Hammerschaimb, *Some Aspects of OT Prophecy from Isaiah to Malachi* (Copenhagen: Rosenkilde Og Bagger, 1966), p. 97.

[149]Daniel K. Smith, *The Religion of the Landless: The Social Context of the Babylonian Exile* (Bloomington, Indiana: Meyer Stone, 1989), p. 11.

[150]Ibid., pp. 139-142. Smith was careful to acknowledge that the P material was a redaction of a significantly developed legal tradition in Israel, not an *ex nihilo* creation of the fifth or sixth century.

[151]Ibid., pp. 148-149.

The impact of this mindset on the reestablishment of the sacrificial cult during the Restoration will be discussed in the analysis of texts from Ezra and Nehemiah.

Introduction to Ezra and Nehemiah

Because Ezra 1-6 is understood to be an independent unit, the critical issues relating to this section will be discussed after those relating to Ezra and Nehemiah as a whole.

The major critical issues related to Ezra and Nehemiah were discussed in chapter one of this study. Before interpreting specific texts it is necessary to indicate the positions assumed on such issues as date and authorship. Dating Ezra and Nehemiah is an immensely complicated task. The final forms of the books, of course, cannot have been produced until after the careers of Ezra and Nehemiah. This would put their earliest possible date in the late fifth century if the early date for Ezra is accepted, and the mid fourth century if the late date is chosen. The inclusion of Jaddua in the list of high priests in Nehemiah 12 would put the earliest possible date at about 400. Williamson has contended that all of the materials regarding Ezra and Nehemiah were compiled at approximately this time, while Ezra 1-6 was added about a century later.[152] Williamson does allow that all of the sources for Ezra and Nehemiah were written "more or less contemporary with the events they relate."[153] The textual history proposed by Cross placed the date of Ezra 1-3 with the first edition of Chronicles in about 520, the rest of Ezra at the middle of the fifth century, and Nehemiah at the end of the fifth

---

[152]H. G. M. Williamson, *Ezra-Nehemiah*, WBC (Waco, Texas: Word Publishing, 1985), p. xxxvi. Williamson's primary argument for the late date of Ezra 1-6 is that the repatriation list in Ezra 2 is dependent upon the similar list found in Nehemiah 7. This point has been refuted recently by Joseph Blenkinsopp, *Ezra Nehemiah*, OTL (Philadelphia: Westminster Press, 1988), p. 43.

[153]Williamson, *Ezra-Nehemiah*, p. xxxv.

century.[154] The final composition of Ezra and Nehemiah probably did occur in about 400. More important for this study is the date of the composition of Ezra 1-6, which will be discussed in the next section.

The extensive use of sources makes the designation of an "author" for Ezra and Nehemiah quite tenuous. Sympathy throughout these two works resided with the returned community. An intense interest in cult and ritual, as in Chronicles, points to the clerical community. Thus, a vague description of a redactor at the end of the fifth century who saw himself as a descendent of those returned from the Exile, and who had close ties to the priesthood is probably the best possible speculation about "authorship" of the works as a whole.

Ezra 1-6 is an extremely complicated piece of literature. It may be outlined as follows.

I.   1:1-4 The Edict of Cyrus

II. 1:5-11 Return under Sheshbazzar

III. 2:1-70 Return under Zerubbabel

IV. 3:1-6 Reinstitution of Worship

V.   3:7-13 Laying of the Temple Foundations

VI. 4:1-5 Conflict with the People of the Land

VII. 4:6-24 A Letter to Artaxerxes and his Reply

VIII. 5:1-5 Beginning the Building of the Temple

IX. 5:6-17 A Letter from Tattenai to Darius

X.   6:1-12 The Decree from Darius

XI. 6:13-15 Finishing the Temple

XII. 6:16-18 Dedication of the Temple

XIII. 6:19-22 Celebration of Passover

---

[154] Frank M. Cross, "A Reconstruction of the Judean Restoration," *JBL*, 94 (1975), 13-15. Others would extend the original work up through Ezra 6. See Geo Widengren, "The Persian Period," in *Israelite and Judean History*, ed. John H. Hayes and J. Maxwell Miller, OTL (Philadelphia: Westminster Press, 1977), p. 504.

A few of these sections stand out as derived primarily from source materials available to the editor. These sources include the Cyrus edict in 1:2-4, the temple inventory in 1:9-11, and the repatriation list in chapter 2. In addition 4:6-6:12 consists mostly of Aramaic documents, with a few verses of narrative framework added.[155] The only large blocks of narrative material provided by the editor, or taken from a source other than those mentioned, are 3:1-4:5 and 6:13-22.[156] These brief portions contain descriptions of three sacrificial events.[157]

There are some chronological problems related to the literary interpretation of the Restoration found in Ezra 1-6. First there is the conflict between 3:8 and 5:16 as to whether it was Zerubbabel or Sheshbazzar who first laid the foundations of the temple in 537. This is explained easily enough

---

[155]See Williamson, *Ezra-Nehemiah*, pp. xxiii-xxiv, and Blenkinsopp, *Ezra-Nehemiah*, p. 42. The entry of the compiler into Aramaic (the official language of the Persian court) at 4:8, and the exit back into Hebrew at 6:19 is something of a mystery. Certainly, the language shift provided an element of authenticity to the documents, but why were the editor's own narrative frameworks in Aramaic? A convincing answer has been provided by Bill T. Arnold, "Bilingualism in Ezra and Daniel," (Unpublished paper delivered at the Society of Biblical Literature, November 23, 1991). Using the literary concept known as "point-of-view," Arnold demonstrated that the shifts in language in Ezra mark shifts in perspective. Once the editor began using an Aramaic source in 4:8 he was committed to a Persian point-of-view, rather than the Jerusalem point-of-view operative up until that point. Only when the issue of rebuilding the temple was completely resolved by its dedication in 6:18 could the editor change points-of-view and languages again.

[156]Some discussion has taken place concerning whether Zechariah 1-6 was used as a source for Ezra 3. See Halpern, *A Historiographic Commentary*, pp. 98-101, David L. Petersen, "Zechariah's Visions: A Theological Perspective," *VT*, 34 (1984), 195-198, and H. G. M. Williamson, "The Composition of Ezra i-vi," *JTS*, 33 (1983), 23-26. The debate has been between Halpern and Petersen (Halpern mistakenly read into Williamson's article the identification of Zechariah as a source for Ezra 3). Halpern pointed to temple reconstruction in Zachariah (such as in 1:16) and an abundance of cultic imagery to make a connection with Ezra 3. Petersen argued that the direct references to temple construction are in the oracular material and not in the visions themselves, and that not all the cultic imagery is related to temple construction. On the whole there appears to be too little direct evidence to declare Zechariah a definite source for Ezra 3. On the other hand, Petersen's claim that there is no connection between the two is a weak overstatement.

[157]See Adam C. Welch, *Post-Exilic Judaism* (London: William Blackwood & Sons, 1935), pp. 158-159. Welch noted that what was certainly a long and complex process of restoration was "telescoped" in Ezra in a fashion similar to the settlement narrative in Joshua.

by the supposition that Zerubbabel led the people in this act under the governorship of Sheshbazzar. Consequently, the laying of the foundations could have been attributed to either.[158] Second, the books of Haggai and Zechariah appear to portray a fresh start on the temple by Zerubbabel in the second year of Darius (520). W. E. Hogg has argued that the meaning of Haggai 2:18 is ambiguous. The work done on the foundations is described by the verb root י ס ד .[159] This could mean they "laid" the foundations, making a fresh start; but it could also mean they "restored" the foundations, building upon previous work.[160] Williamson has attempted to establish, on literary grounds, that the book of Ezra does not portray an early beginning on the temple in the time of Cyrus, but that 3:7-4:3 describes the activity in the time of Darius.[161] Unfortunately, Williamson's argument is a bit unclear here, and this explanation substitutes an extremely convoluted reading for the plain meaning of the text. Baruch Halpern took this line of argument a great deal further, recognizing that the editor intended to imply a chronology in which those returning under Zerubbabel in 538 began rebuilding the temple in 537, but were delayed by opposition until 520. Thus, there was no apparent lack of diligence among the returnees as implied in Haggai 2. Halpern further suggested that the editor created a "dual sequence" which did not destroy the "real chronology" in which Zerubbabel returned in 520, long after the first return and altar building, to oversee the rebuilding of the temple. Halpern

---

[158]Williamson, *Ezra-Nehemiah*, p. 43.

[159]This root is also used to describe Zerubbabel's work in Ezra 3:10. Petersen has described an ancient Mesopotamian building ritual in which a stone from a previous building is placed in a new building. This fits well with Haggai 2:15. Thus, regardless of whether Zerubbabel began rebuilding in 537, 520, or both, he did not necessarily rebuild from nothing.

[160]W. E. Hogg, "The Founding of the Second Temple," *PTR*, 25 (1927), 458.

[161]Williamson, *Ezra-Nehemiah*, pp. 43-44. Williamson's position is based on Shemaryahu Talmon's description of Ezra 4:4-5 as a "summary notation." See Shemaryahu Talmon, "Ezra and Nehemiah," in *The Interpreter's* Dictionary of the Bible: Supplementary Volume, ed. Keith Crim (Nashville: Abingdon, 1976), p. 323.

concluded that the organizing principle of Ezra 1-6 is "subject matter, not chronology."[162] Likewise, this is a rather complex reading of a relatively simple narrative. The confusion lies in trying to square it with external historical data and other biblical material.

This study will proceed on the basis that Ezra 1-6 presents a straightforward, literary interpretation of the Restoration in which the exiles returned under threatening conditions; but through faithful performance of the sacrificial cult they engendered the favor of God and established a stable, worshiping community. As in the latter portions of Chronicles, there appears in Ezra 1-6 an urgent need both to interpret the Exile and establish the validity of the restoration carried out by the returnees. This agenda, along with the connecting of the second temple cult with that of Solomon's temple, would seem to suit the needs of the community early in the restoration process. Therefore, a late sixth or early fifth century date for Ezra 1-6 will be assumed as a working hypothesis. Before proceeding with the discussion of the relevant passages from this section, an examination of the condition of the temple and the sacrificial cult during the Exile will provide a more complete backdrop for understanding the interpretation of the restoration of worship these texts provide.

As at the end of Chronicles, the concentatration of sacrificial events in the first half of Ezra is high. This is especially true when the inserted source documents are removed and only the narrative framework is considered.

---

[162]Baruch Halpern, "A Historiographic Commentary on Ezra 1-6: A Chronological Narrative and Dual Chronology in Israelite History," in *The Hebrew Bible and Its Interpreters*, ed. William Henry Propp, et al. (Winona Lake, Indiana: Eisenbrauns, 1990), p. 113.

The Reinstitution of Worship and

Conflict with the People of the Land

Ezra 3:1-6 and 4:1-5

3:1 The seventh month came and the people of Israel were in the cities. Then the people gathered together in Jerusalem. 2 Jeshua, son of Jozadek, rose up, and his brothers the priests and Zerubbabel, son of Shealtiel, and his brothers, to restore the altar of the God of Israel; to offer unto him a burnt offering as written in the law of Moses, the man of God. 3 They established the altar on its foundations[163] because of the dread[164] upon them from the peoples of the lands; and they offered up upon it burnt offerings to the Lord, burnt offerings for the morning and for the evening. 4 They celebrated the festival of Booths as it is written, and a burnt offering[165] day by day, by number according to the ordinance, each one on its own day. 5 Then afterwards a burnt offering regularly, and at the new moons, and for all the festivals of the Lord, the holy ones, and for every one offering a free-will offering to the Lord. 6 From the first day of the seventh month they began to offer burnt offerings to the Lord, but they did not establish the temple.

4:1 When the enemies of Judah and Benjamin heard that the children of the Exile were building the temple of the Lord, the God of Israel, 2 they approached Zerubbabel[166] and the heads of the fathers and said to them,"Let us build with you, for like you we seek your God. We have been sacrificing to him[167] from the days of Esarhaddon, king of Assyria, the one bringing us here. 3 But Zerubbabel and Jeshua and the rest of the fathers of Israel said to them, "It is not for you and for us together to build the house of our God. For we alone shall build for the LORD, the God of Israel, as

---

[163]LXX has the singular "foundation."

[164]LXX has "enmity," probably based on an emendation changing the MT ב א י מ ה to
ב א י ב ה .

[165]LXX has the plural "burnt offerings."

[166]LXX adds "and Jeshua."

[167]This translation is based on the *qere* ו ל ו instead of ו ל א in the text. Another alternative is to read the *kethib* as an emphatic use of ל א , rather than a negative.

Cyrus, the King of Persia commanded us. 4 And the people of the land were weakening the hands of the people of Judah and making them frightened to build. 5 They hired against them counselors to frustrate their plan, all the days of Cyrus until the kingdom of Darius, King of Persia.

Ezra 3:1-4:5 narrates the attempt of the returned community to restore the Jerusalem cult. Three separate episodes took place. First, they reconstructed the altar and offered sacrifices upon it. Second, they laid the foundations of the temple and celebrated. Third, the surrounding peoples came asking to join in the work, were refused, and acted to thwart the building process. The first of these episodes is the overt sacrificial event. The third is also included in the analysis here because it accomplished the cessation of the cultic renewal, and for other reasons that will become apparent later.[168]

Ezra 3:1-6 describes the actions of the returnees soon after they arrived in Palestine. They set up the altar and began a regular program of sacrifices. In this description the editor denied even the existence of a sacrificial cult during the Exile. Its legitimacy is even further from consideration.[169] At the same time, the editor wished to establish a connection with pre-Exilic worship. Hence, the importance of building the new altar "on its foundations," implying that it was put where the former altar had stood and that the old altar was no more.[170] By making this a dedication of a new altar on the old site the editor asserted that it was the group returning from Babylon which was the true heir of the Israelite relationship with God.[171] In these few verses the author set up a delicate sense of tension between

---

[168]This event provides evidence of conflict in post-Exilic Palestine. It is often used in discussions of the development of the Samaritan schism.

[169]See Welch, *Post-Exilic Judaism*, pp. 160-161 and Janssen, *Juda in der Exilsheit*, p. 101.

[170]Blenkinsopp, *Ezra-Nehemiah*, p. 97.

[171]Williamson, *Ezra-Nehemiah*, p. 46.

62

discontinuity which he would seek to maintain throughout the remainder of Ezra 1-6.

The motivation for setting up the altar in 3:3, described in a remarkable statement, was fear of the "peoples of the lands" (עם י הארצות). It is not immediately obvious to whom this expression refers. Its meaning must be considered in conjunction with the singular expression עם האר ץ in Ezra 4:4.[172] The simplest explanation is that the peoples in 3:3 are outside groups that had been Israel's traditional enemies,[173] while the singular group in 4:4 refers to the other people within Palestine who were not with the returnees.[174] If this understanding is correct then in 3:3 the community was afraid of outside attack. They apparently believed that by building the altar and carrying on the sacrificial cult they could acquire divine protection from their enemies.[175] The Exile must have loomed large in their minds. They did not want to suffer a recurrence of such devastation. If this was the motivation of the early post-Exilic community, then it is clear that they understood the lack of proper sacrifice as the cause of the Exile. Such is the picture that the editor of Ezra 1-6 painted.

The editor's assertion that this entire performance was carried out by a unified community, as stated in 3:1, is also of significance. Indeed, Halpern has suggested that 3:1-6 has been entirely reordered to place v. 1 before vv. 2-3, so that the gathered people were identified as the builders of the new

---

[172]See Ernest W. Nicholson, "The Meaning of the Expression *'m h'rts* in the Old Testament," *JSS*, 10 (1965), 66. In a definitive article Nicholson argued that this expression has "no fixed and rigid meaning but is used rather in a purely general and fluid manner and varies in meaning from context to context. Nicholson did not discuss specifically the plural expression as it is found in Ezra 3:3.

[173]See Blenkinsopp, *Ezra-Nehemiah*, p. 98. Blenkinsopp suggests the Edomites as a possibility here.

[174]Nicholson, "The Expression *'m h'rts*," p. 66. Nicholson noted that in 4:4 the phrase is contrasted with "people of Judah."

[175]Williamson, *Ezra-Nehemiah*, p. 46.

altar. If the original verse order was 2-3-1, as Halpern supposed, then the people would have gathered for the festival after the building of the altar and offering of the initial sacrifices were already accomplished.[176] Whether or not Halpern's reconstruction is correct, it was obviously important to the editor that this was a unified action of the whole community.

After the subsequent laying of the foundations, another group approached the leaders of the returnees desiring inclusion in the activity of restoring the temple cult. These claimed to have been continuing the sacrificial cult since they had been relocated in Judah by the Assyrians. Zerubbabel and Jeshua rejected them, however, creating the opposition which halted the plans to build the temple.[177] Assuming that "the people of the land" in 4:4 refers back to those in 4:1, the building of the temple was delayed by internal tensions within Judah.[178] There is a curious contradiction between the episodes in 3:1-6 and 4:1-5. The same group of people who had begun restoring the sacrificial cult out of fear of the "peoples of the lands" chose to stop shortly afterward out of fear of the "people of the land."[179]

Before proceeding with any interpretation of this event it seems necessary to explore the difficult, related passage in Haggai 2:10-14. Both passages refer to the period of temple rebuilding and the difficulties

---

[176]Halpern, *A Historiographic Commentary*, p. 94.

[177]This is a questionable position, requiring the identification of the "people of the land" in 4:4 with the enemies in 4:1, but it seems to fit the plain meaning of the Ezra narrative.

[178]This is the assumption of D. J. A. Clines (*Ezra, Nehemiah, Esther*, NCBC, [Grand Rapids, Michigan: Wm. B. Eerdmans, 1984], pp. 72-73). The connection of the groups mentioned in 4:1 and 4:4, however, is not a certainty. See Blenkinsopp, *Ezra-Nehemiah*, p. 108. It is difficult, however, to divorce 4:1-3 from 4:4-5 in a straight-forward reading of the text. Regardless of the actual historical events behind the situation, Ezra 3:1-4:5 presents a continuous narrative. What happened in 4:4-5 appears to be the result of the events in 4:1-3.

[179]This contradiction usually receives little, if any, attention. See Williamson, *Ezra-Nehemiah*, p. 46 and Blenkinsopp, *Ezra-Nehemiah*, p. 108.

experienced by the community during that time. They are, however, translucent interpretations of the situation, offering very little in the way of direct historical information. The event in Haggai 2 is clearly placed within the period of temple building in 520. The priests were called together and questioned about the contagion of both holiness and uncleanness. The essence of their answer was that holiness is not transferrable from one object to another, while uncleanness is. The verse following this ruling, Haggai 2:14, is one of the most puzzling in all of the Bible. After the priests' answer Haggai said, "'Thus is this people and thus is this nation,' says the Lord, 'and thus is all the work of their hands; and what they offer there is unclean.'" The primary difficulty is the appearance of העם הזה (this people) and הגוי הזה (this nation) side-by-side. The foremost question is whether these phrases refer to two groups of people or just one. If two, then are they the same groups which were interacting in Ezra 4:1-5?[180] There are other occasions in the Hebrew Bible where the Hebrew people are referred to as גוי, though the more common designation is עם.[181]

---

[180]This issue was complicated considerably by the assertion of Rothstein many years ago that Ezra 4:1-5 and Haggai 2:10-14 were the basis of the Samaritan schism. See J. W. Rothstein, *Juden und Samaritaner: Die Grundlegende Scheidung von Judentum und Heidentum* (Leipzig: J. C. Heinrichs, 1908), pp. 40-41. A predominance of more recent research has concluded that there are no references to the Samaritans in the sixth century prophetic material. See R. J. Coggins, *Samaritans and Jews: The Origins of Samaritanism Reconsidered* (Atlanta: John Knox Press, 1975), p. 56 and H. G. May, "'This People' and 'This Nation' in Haggai," *VT*, 18 (1968), 192. A notable exception is the recent work of H. Werner Wolff. Wolff, following Rothstein, argued against Petersen and Coggins, asserting that it was improbable for the two phrases in Haggai 2:14 to refer to the same groups. The event recorded, therefore, does refer to the Samaritan expulsion. H. Werner Wolff, *Haggai* (Minneapolis: Augsburg Publishing, 1988), pp. 92-94. The denial of a reference to the Samaritans does not mean that there was no class conflict within Judah during this period. See Daniel L. Smith, *The Religion of the Landless*, p. 184; and Morton Smith, *Palestinian Parties and Politics that Shaped the Old Testament* (London: SCM Press, 1987), p. 86. Morton Smith has argued that an alliance between the Jerusalem priesthood and what he calls the "Yahweh-alone" party, led by Zerubbabel, took place in the late sixth century, excluding other residents of Palestine. The conflict created by this action is likely reflected in Ezra 4:1-5.

[181]See A. Cody, "When Is the Chosen People Called a *Goy*," *VT*, 14 (1964), 1-2. Cody identified several contexts in which Israel was designated in this way, two of which may apply to Haggai 2:14. One possible context is in a statement of rejection by God. A second is in the context of taking territory, thus becoming a landed nation. Either possibility could be made to

The conclusion of May, Coggins, and Petersen that only one group is referred to in Haggai 2:14 leads to the question of the source of the unclean mentioned in this verse. May asserted that Israel had become unclean through failure to devote proper attention to the temple.[182] On the other hand, Petersen aptly pointed out that nothing is said about people being unclean. What was unclean was "the work of their hands," the produce which they were bringing to the temple as offerings and sacrifices. How could every offering be unclean? For the questioning of the priests to make sense, the produce must have become unclean by contact with a defiled object. Petersen contended that this object was the temple or, specifically, the altar itself. It was impure because it had not been properly dedicated.[183]

In Haggai 2:10-14 there is no clear sense of one group being chosen and another being rejected, or of one group excluding another. Thus, there is no definite parallel to Ezra 4:1-5. There is, however, a common theme. The reestablishment of sacrificial worship must be done in a careful and proper manner to avoid impurity. Defilement might occur from inclusion of unclean peoples, but it could also come from the improper conduct of those who were rightfully included.

In Ezra 4:1-5 the concern for purity brought about the rejection of another group of people. This episode along with the altar building in Ezra 3:1-6, placed as they are, highlight the editor's concern for proper sacrificial worship. Such worship was vital for the divine protection of the community from the threat of outside invasion. Polluted sacrifice offered an even greater threat, however. Those returning from the Exile insisted upon an exclusive

---

fit this passage.

[182]May. "'This People' and 'This Nation' in Haggai," p. 196.

[183]David L. Petersen, *Haggai and Zechariah 1-8*, OTL (Philadelphia: Westminster Press, 1984), pp. 80-85. Petersen's conclusion was based on an extensive analysis of the purity and impurity terms used in Haggai and the understanding of contagion in Israel's law codes. His argument is quite convincing, but it depends on a quite different understanding of the Exile in Haggai than that which appears in Ezra. This will be discussed in a later section.

inheritance of the sacrificial cult. Thus, they were willing to jeopardize the continuation of their program by the exclusion of other inhabitants of Judah. That they did not trust the favor of God acquired by their renewal in 3:1-6 to protect them in the conflict presented in 4:1-5 might indicate that the fear of internal strife was much greater than that of foreign invasion. The full resolution of this problem would have to wait until the events at the end of Ezra 6, after the completion of all the political machinations between the Persian empire and the Judean province.

The Dedication of the New Temple
Ezra 6:16-18

16 The children of Israel, the priests, the Levites, and the rest of the children of the Exile, celebrated the dedication of the house of God[184] with joy. 17 They offered at the dedication of the house of God this: 100 bulls, 200 rams, 400 lambs, and he-goats as a sin offering for all Israel - twelve for the number of the tribes of Israel. 18 They established the priests in their divisions and the Levites in their courses for the service of God who is in Jerusalem, according to the book of Moses.

At the dedication of the newly finished second temple another overt sacrificial event took place. The report of this event contains some of the elements common to sacrificial narratives of Chronicles, but most of the graphic detail is absent. The most important previous account to compare with Ezra 6:16-18 is the dedication of Solomon's temple in II Chronicles 7.[185] In addition, of course, a parallel narrative of Ezra 6:16-18 appears in I Esdras 7:6-9. Perhaps the most mysterious aspect of this passage is that is in the Aramaic language, even though the editor had finished quoting

---

[184]MT adds a seemingly unnecessary demonstrative ה נ ד . LXX and Vulgate omit it.

[185]R. J. Coggins, *The Books of Ezra and Nehemiah*, TCBC (Cambridge: Cambridge University Press, 1976), p. 40.

Aramaic documents and had begun providing his own narrative.[186] The proposal of Arnold that the changes in language represent changes in point-of-view is quite convincing. If this is correct, then in 6:16-18 the editor was still writing from a Persian point-of-view, even though the official Aramaic documents had been completed.[187] The rebuilding had been ordered in the decree of Darius. Therefore, this was, at least indirectly, a Persian project.

If Ezra 6:16-18 reflects Solomon's temple dedication in II Chronicles 7, then Ezra 1-6 may be understood as something of a reversal of the downhill slide to destruction presented in the latter parts of Chronicles. Israel was returned to its Solomonic conditions. Likewise, it had returned to the days of Josiah and Hezekiah, who was clearly pictured as a second Solomon. The number of sacrificial offerings at the dedication of the second temple were nowhere near the magnitude of those in Solomon's dedication. Nevertheless, specific numbers are supplied by the text. Assuming the numbers in II Chronicles 7 were accurate,[188] it would be hard to imagine that the returned community, still in the early stages of economic recovery, would have been capable of offering up animals by the tens of thousands. Still, the editor was concerned with at least some of the specifics of the sacrificial ceremony.

The narrative in Ezra 6:16-18 also contains important parallels to the altar dedication and the starting of the temple in Ezra 3. The list of participants in 6:16 reflects that found in 3:8, while the claim to be following the book of Moses in 6:18 matches such statements in 3:2 and 3:4. The use of ה נ ל ב (division) and ה ק ל ח מ (course) for groupings of the priests and Levites may serve to connect Ezra 6:16-18 with the Passover of Josiah in II Chronicles

---

[186]Williamson, *Ezra-Nehemiah*, pp. 73-74, 84. Williamson argued correctly that the change to Aramaic in no way indicates a change in authorship or the constraint of any source. For a contrary explanation, see D. J. A. Clines, *Ezra, Nehemiah, Esther*, pp. 94-96.

[187]Arnold, "Bilingualism in Ezra and Daniel."

[188]Recall that zeroes were very likely added to the end of the numbers in II Chronicles 7 to provide an exaggerated effect. See J. W. Wenham, "Large Numbers in the Old Testament," *TynB*, 18 (1967), 49.

35:4-5.[189]   Therefore, this very brief account contains links to Solomon's temple dedication, Hezekiah's reform, Josiah's reform, and the original reinstitution of worship in Ezra 3. As in the great sacrificial events of the past, there is emphasis here on the united participation of "the people of Israel" for whom twelve goats were offered "according to the number of the tribes of Israel" (6:17-18). The finishing touches of this new venture would be provided by the Passover celebration to follow.

The Restoration Passover
Ezra 6:19-22

> The exiles celebrated the Passover on the fourteenth of the first month,   20 for the priests and the Levites had made all of them pure.[190]   They killed the Passover lamb for all the children of the Exile and for their brothers, the priests, and for themselves. 21 The children of Israel ate,[191] the ones returning from the Exile, and all separating themselves from the impurity of the nations of the land to seek the Lord, the God of Israel. 22 They celebrated the feast of the Unleavened Bread seven days with gladness; for the Lord made them joyful, and he turned the heart of the king of Assyria unto them to strengthen their hands in the work of the house of God,[192] the God of Israel.

By concluding with this account of the Passover, the editor of Ezra 1-6 accomplished a number of important literary tasks. First, he reverted back to the Hebrew language in 6:19 so that the point-of-view was once again Jerusalem, not Persia.[193]   Second, he connected the first event of the new

---

[189]Blenkinsopp, *Ezra-Nehemiah*, pp. 130-131.

[190]LXXa adds "as one."

[191]LXX adds "the Passover."

[192]LXXa, Vulgate, and Syriac replace "God" with "the Lord."

[193]Arnold, "Bilingualism in Ezra and Daniel."

temple with the great Passover celebrations of Josiah and Hezekiah. Third, the Passover, presented as a pilgrimage festival centralized in Jerusalem, brought together "the people of Israel" (6:21) in a defining moment. Finally, by making the statement concerning the Lord's influence on the king in 16:22 he neatly concluded the narrative begun in Ezra 1:1.[194] In order to understand the powerful effect of these few verses, each of these elements will be examined below in further detail.

The establishment of the restored sacrificial cult was surely a long and trying process. It involved not only the will of the returned community, but also the sponsorship of the ruling Persian government. As mentioned earlier, a Persian point-of-view was created by the use of the Aramaic language, not only in the official documents in Ezra 4-6, but also in the narrative framework surrounding them.[195] From Ezra 4:8-6:18 the outcome of events was in the hands of the empire. Once the temple was completed and dedicated, however, the operating of the sacrificial cult was in the hands of the restored community. The return to the Hebrew language and, therefore, a Jerusalem point-of-view in 6:19-22 signaled this victory and provided a fitting end to the editor's story. Once again, a profound moment was marked by the performance of a sacrificial ritual.

The description of the Passover in Ezra 6:19-22 lacks the grandeur of the accounts in II Chronicles 30 (Hezekiah) and II Chronicles 35 (Josiah).[196] The Restoration Passover does have a marked number of similarities to these earlier celebrations, however. It was celebrated in Jerusalem by a unified community on the fourteenth day of the first month, and it was linked

---

[194]Clines, *Ezra, Nehemiah, Esther*, p. 98.

[195]Arnold, "Bilingualism in Ezra and Daniel."

[196]Recall the possibility proposed in the previous chapter that the purpose of tremendous detail in the reports of sacrificial events in the latter parts of II Chronicles was to provide indirect detail for the slaughter (sacrifice) of the young people of Israel in II Chronicles 36:17. If this is true, then such a purpose would not be present in Ezra 6. This editor had a different agenda.

together with the festival of Unleavened Bread which continued for seven days afterward. Also, the Levites were responsible for the slaughtering of the Passover lamb.[197] As in the accounts in Chronicles, this Passover in Ezra was based on a compilation of legal codes, rather than one specific tradition from the Torah.[198] The editor portrayed a unified sacrificial event, making use of a variety of traditions.[199]

The Hebrew narrative in Ezra 3:1-4:7 is filled with conflict and tension. In 6:21 this conflict appears to be resolved. The group which had inherited the cultic traditions of Israel had been decided, though the demarcations were not entirely clear. What is clear is that, for at least a moment, persons who had not been in exile were allowed entrance into the community. Just who were "all separating themselves from the impurity of the nations of the land unto them to seek the Lord, the God of Israel?" This designation may have included one or more of the following groups present in Judah: (1) The Judeans who had not been exiled, (2) Northern Israelites who had remained in Samaria after the Assyrian invasion of the eighth century or had moved south into Judah, and (3) foreigners who may have been brought in by the Assyrians to settle Israel.[200] One cannot be certain, but the first of these

---

[197]Judson R. Shaver, *Torah and the Chronicler's History Work: An Inquiry into the Chronicler's Reference to Laws, Festivals and Cultic Institutions in Relationship to Pentateuchal Legislation* (Atlanta: Scholar's Press, 1989), pp. 116-117.

[198]Ibid., p. 117.

[199]The lack of a statement similar to those in II Chronicles 30:9 and 35:18, about when the last Passover like this was kept is a bit disturbing. Could it be that a knowledge of Kings or Chronicles was assumed and, thus, the reader would know that the last great Passover was Josiah's? On the other hand, could the lack of a statement of superiority by the editor be a silent admission that this Passover was not grand by pre-Exilic standards, due to the conditions in post-Exilic Judah?

[200]Sara Japhet, "People and Land in the Restoration Period," in *Das Land Israel in Biblischer Zeit*, ed. Georg Strecker (Göttingen: Vandenhoeck & Ruprecht, 1983), pp. 104-105. The existence of the last of these three groups is debatable. In any case, they would seem to be the least likely to have been accepted into the Restoration community. See Williamson, *Ezra-Nehemiah*, p. 85. Williamson contended, however, that the group should be understood as proselytes.

groups must have been allowed to join the Restoration community. Openness to the latter two groups seems less likely, but is still a possibility.

The text in 6:21 is not specific at all about who joined the returnees. There are indications, though, that membership was not entirely open. There is fairly solid evidence that the repatriation lists in Ezra 2, Nehemiah 7, and I Esdras 5 were constructed to legitimize the restored community, with names being added where necessary. Individuals had to get their names on the list to gain membership. According to Japhet, the purpose of the list was "to consider all the people of Judah, whether or not they went into exile, as returnees."[201]

As Daniel L. Smith concluded, all of the evidence related to the repatriation lists indicates that the Restoration period was a time of great social instability.[202] The resulting conflict is apparent in Ezra 4:1-5. Once the temple was operating, however, a source of identity was found in the sacrificial cult. According to Ezra 6:21 one unified worshiping community was formed.

Ezra 6:22 closes the Passover and the entire story in Ezra 1-6. As with the Passovers of Hezekiah and Josiah, Unleavened Bread was observed for the seven days following. Israel was a restored worshiping community. The statement that the Lord "had turned the heart of the King of Assyria to them" almost certainly forms an inclusio with the statement in Ezra 1:1 that "the Lord stirred up the spirit of King Cyrus of Persia." The obvious problem is the reference to Assyria, since Darius must be the king to whom 6:22 refers. The standard explanation is that because the Persians were the

---

[201]Japhet, "People and Land in the Restoration Period," p. 114. See Wilhelm Rudolph, *Esra und Nehemiah* (Tübingen: Verlag J. C. B. Mohr, 1949), pp. 19-20. Rudolph pointed to the change from ׳ ﬨ ﬨ (sons of) to ׳ ﬐ ﬡ (men of) as evidence of additions to the lists (see Ezra 2:23). See the excellent discussion of this entire issue by Daniel L. Smith, *The Religion of the Landless*, pp. 103-106. The sociology of the Restoration period will be discussed more extensively in the next chapter.

[202]Smith, *The Religion of the Landless*, p. 106.

successors of the Assyrians, by way of the Babylonians, these conquering empires were synonymous in Israel's thought. This understanding of the reference seems likely enough, though certainty cannot be achieved on this issue.[203] Thus, the four Hebrew verses at the end of chapter 6 provide proper closure and serve as a fitting end to a complete narrative.

The Theology of Sacrifice in Ezra 1-6

A discussion of the theology of sacrifice may at first seem improper for a document of this length which contains descriptions of only three sacrificial events. One must remember, however, that if the obvious source documents are discounted these three accounts form a large majority of the editor's narrative material. In fact, of the four events in Palestine reported in Ezra 1-6, three were overtly sacrificial. The editor of Ezra 1-6 appears to have been concerned with three major issues of the restored cult. First, a tension had to be maintained between continuity and discontinuity with the past. Second, faithful sacrifice was necessary to guarantee the survival of the community. Third, this sacrificial cult had to be carried out by a pure, but eventually unified, people of Israel. The experience of exile was intimately connected to all of these issues.

The impression provided by Ezra 1-6 is that no religious activity took place in Jerusalem from the dreadful day in 586 when the temple was burned until the construction of the new altar in Ezra 3:1-6. This gap placed a clean break between the first temple and the second. At the same time, continuity is established by several elements of the story. According to 3:3, the returnees built the new altar on the foundations of the old altar. The temple dedication in 6:16-18 parallels the dedication of the first temple in several

---

[203] For examples of this line of reasoning, see Williamson, *Ezra-Nehemiah*, p. 85 and Blenkinsopp, *Ezra-Nehemiah*, p. 133. There is always the possibility, however remote, that the reference to Assyria is a scribal error.

ways. The observance of Passover in 6:19-22 ties the activity of the second temple to that of the first in the great reform days of Hezekiah and Josiah. The new cult is connected to the best elements of the old, with the worst of its history entirely ignored. Rex Mason has explained the focus on cultic concerns in Chronicles, Ezra, and Nehemiah on the basis of a need for continuity: "...when their [the people of Israel] existence can no longer be guaranteed in political terms, the continuity of the outward forms and institutions of their faith ... become all important."[204]

The returnees began to offer sacrifices almost immediately upon their return to Palestine. It was more urgent than the physical rebuilding of the temple. Ezra 3:3 reports that the sense of urgency was created by fear of the surrounding peoples. This group which had just returned from exile wanted, more than anything else, the assurance that they would not be carried off again. That this was the fear that made them set up the altar and begin sacrificing is the only explanation that makes sense in the light of Ezra 4:1-5. Internal threats of disruption and contamination brought the Restoration program to a halt. After the dispute had been settled through diplomatic channels, the Restoration was continued. The message of the seventh century reform movements was clear. God's favor is the result of a properly conducted sacrificial cult.

Some misconceptions about sacrifice in Ezra 1-6 need to be cleared up here. In these chapters there is no indication that the returnees were trying to atone for the sins of the past. There is no reference to pre-Exilic unfaithfulness or contamination of the temple site.[205] The temple site was not in need of purification from past evils. The sacrificial offerings in Ezra

---

[204]Rex Mason, *Preaching the Tradition: Homily and Hermeneutics after the Exile* (Cambridge: Cambridge University Press, 1990), pp. 260-262.

[205]This is the position of F. C. Fensham ("Some Theological and Religious Aspects in Ezra and Nehemiah," *JNSL*, 11 [1983], 64). He claimed that "... a sense of guilt for the sins committed just before the destruction of the temple was still strongly felt in the time of Ezra." Whether or not this is true in the time of Ezra, there is no hint of it in Ezra 1-6.

6:17 are similar to those offered at Solomon's dedication. They appear to have been standard offerings for the dedication of a temple. Even the statement of Clines that the sin offerings in 6:17 were offered "to decontaminate the temple or altar from any impurity brought upon it during its building" is clearly a mis-reading.[206] The text plainly says that the twelve male goats were a sin offering "for all Israel." In addition, the background of the sin offering in Leviticus 4:23 and 9:3 indicates that this offering was to cleanse people not places.

The primary accomplishment of Ezra 1-6 emerges in the final two verses. The people of Israel had become a unified, worshiping community. Tamara Eskenazi has identified an emphasis on community achievement throughout Ezra and Nehemiah, at the expense of the glorification of leaders. The roles of the leaders are "submerged." Ezra 6:16-22, which does not refer to any person by name, epitomizes this perspective of the editor. At the temple dedication the names of Zerubbabel and Sheshbazzar are conspicuously absent. At the Passover there is no leader, unlike the Passover celebrations in Chronicles which were conducted by kings.[207] Could the community based initiative of this renewal be the secret to its lasting success? According to Eskenazi, the community was empowered in Ezra and Nehemiah instead of its leaders.[208] The drawing together of the community in Ezra 6:21 literally undid the Exile. The people had been torn apart and their worship disrupted. The final verses of Ezra 1-6 completed the reversal of these conditions.

---

[206]Clines, *Ezra, Nehemiah, Esther,* p. 96.

[207]Tamara Cohn Eskenazi, *In an Age of Prose: A Literary Approach to Ezra-Nehemiah* (Atlanta: Scholar's Press, 1988), pp. 47-53. Eskenazi also pointed out the departure, in Ezra and Nehemiah, from the tradition of the Ancient Near East as a whole where gods and kings built temples.

[208]Ibid., p. 53.

The Return of Ezra and His Party

Ezra 8:35

35The ones returning from the captivity, the children of the Exile, brought burnt offerings to the God of Israel: twelve bulls for all Israel, ninety-six rams, seventy-seven lambs, and twelve goats for a sin-offering, all as a burnt offering for the Lord.[209]

A final sacrificial event appears in Ezra, outside of the first six chapters. That this event is only one verse long precludes it from being central to the narrative of the second half of the book. It may, however, form a very important addendum to the theology of sacrifice in Ezra 1-6. The group travelling with Ezra arrived back in Jerusalem about sixty years after the original group of returnees.[210] According to this verse, the first action the newly arriving group took was the offering of sacrifices to God.[211] The report of the event is brief, but highly symbolic. All of the numbers of the sacrifices are multiples of twelve, the symbolic number for Israel. The parallels are once again present between this and previous events, such as the the temple dedication in Ezra 6:17 and Hezekiah's dedication in II Chronicles 29:20-24.[212]

This later group of returnees was obeying the orders of Artaxerxes in performing these sacrifices (see Ezra 7:17), just as the original group had built

---

[209]See Norman Snaith, "A Note on Ezra viii.35," *JTS*, 22 (1971), 150-152. Snaith pointed out the problem that sin-offerings were never burnt offerings. Therefore, the last phrase cannot refer to the final element in the list of sacrifices. The simplest solution is to invert the two phrases.

[210]This figure is based on the early date for Ezra's return. The late date would put about 120 years between the two groups of returnees.

[211]It should be noted that the narration changes from first to third person. See Williamson, *Ezra-Nehemiah*, pp. 116,122. Williamson explained this shift by assigning vv 35-36 to the final editor of the Ezra Memoir.

[212]Blenkinsopp, *Ezra-Nehemiah*, p. 173.

the temple according to the command of Darius and had returned to the land according to the decree of Cyrus. More importantly, this act of sacrifice would have functioned to join them with the community already present and dwelling in Palestine. In fact, there is no reason to insist that the term מ הש ב ׳ ה ב א ׳ ם referred only to those who had just returned with Ezra. It may just as easily have referred to the entire Restoration community participating in a joint sacrificial event.

The Dedication of the Wall
Nehemiah 12:27-43

Sacrifice would seem to be a fairly trivial issue in Nehemiah, since there is only one sacrificial event described in the book. An additional issue arises however, from the placement of this event in the book. A broad outline of Nehemiah will help to illustrate the problem.

I. Building of the Wall Around Jerusalem Despite Intense Opposition. (Nehemiah 1:1-7:5a)

II. The Repatriation List. (Nehemiah 7:5b-72a)

III. Reading of the Law and Services of Covenant Renewal. (Nehemiah 7:72b-10:40)

IV. Lists of Settlements and Temple Personnel. (Nehemiah 11:1-12:26)

V. Dedication of the Wall. (Nehemiah 12:27-43)

VI. Additional Reforms. (Nehemiah 12:44-13:31)

Why is the dedication of the wall saved until chapter 12 when it would seem to belong immediately following Nehemiah 7:5a when the wall was completed. The following sections will examine the sacrificial text itself and the problem of its placement within the book.

27 At the dedication of the walls of Jerusalem they sought the Levites from all their places to bring them to Jerusalem to celebrate the dedication with joy, and with thanksgiving, and with singing, cymbals, harps, and lyres. 28 The sons of the singers gathered, from the circuit around Jerusalem and from the villages of the Netophathites. 29 From Beth-Gilgal and the region of Geba and Azmareth, for the singers had built for themselves villages around Jerusalem. 30 The priests and the Levites purified themselves, and they purified the people, the gates, and the wall. 31 I brought up the leaders of Judah on top of the wall, and I appointed two great companies and processions[213] to the right on the wall to the Dung Gate. 32 Hoshaiah went after them and half of the leaders of Judah. 33 Also Azariah, Ezra, and Meshullam, 34 Judah, Benjamin, Shemaiah, and Jeremiah. 35 And some from the sons of the priests with trumpets: Zechariah, son of Johathan, son of Shemaiah, son of Mattaniah, son of Mikaiah, son of Zakkur, son of Asaph. 36 And his brothers Shemaiah, Azarel, Milalai, Gilalai, Masi, Nethanel, Judah, and Hanani with the instruments of the music of David, the man of God. Ezra the scribe was before them. 37 Unto the Fountain Gate in front of them they went up upon the stairs of the city of David at the ascent of the wall, above the house of David to the Water Gate on the east. The second company went to the north[214] and I was behind them, and half of the people on the wall above the Tower of the Ovens to the Broad Wall. 39 Above the Gate of Ephraim to the Gate of Mishneh, and to the Fish Gate, the Tower of Hananel, the Tower of the Hundred to the Sheep Gate, and they stood at the Gate of the Guard. 40 Then the two companies were standing in the house of God, myself and half the officials with me. 41 The priests: Eliakim, Maaseiah, Miniamin, Micaiah, Elioenai, Zecharia, and Hananiah with the trumpets. 42 Maaseiah, Shemaiah, Eleazer, Uzzi, Jehohanan, Malchijah, Elam, Ezer, and the singers sang with Jezrahiah, the leader. 43 They sacrificed great sacrifices on that day, and they rejoiced, for God made them rejoice with great joy. Also the women and children rejoiced, and the joy of Jerusalem was heard from afar.

---

[213]An emendation is often made here causing the text to read "and the one walked off to the right . . . ." There is no textual evidence to support it. See Williamson, *Ezra-Nehemiah*, p. 368.

[214]This translation is based on the addition of a ‫ו‬. For a full discussion, see Williamson, *Ezra-Nehemiah*, p. 368.

These verses contain the only sacrificial ceremony in the book of Nehemiah. The description of the event is obviously quite different from those encountered in Chronicles and Ezra. If the descriptions of sacrifice itself in Chronicles were graphic and those in Ezra understated, then this one is almost an afterthought. There is tremendous detail in the passage, but it focuses on the procession leading up to the sacrificial ritual. The urgency of sacrifice found in Chronicles and Ezra is entirely absent. Sections of Nehemiah 12:27-43 are typically classified as part of the Nehemiah Memoir, which includes the first-person narrative passages in Nehemiah.[215] The portion of the memoir in Nehemiah 12 appears after a lengthy insertion of other material. The editor of Nehemiah chose to place the dedication ceremony for the wall after the covenant renewal in chapters 8-11. The disassociation of the dedication with the completion of the wall will be addressed further in the next section.

As part of a renewal ceremony, the sacrifices in 12:43 do share common features with the great sacrificial events during the days of Hezekiah and Josiah. The author was very concerned with reporting who was present, including, of course, the priests and the Levites. 12:43 places emphasis upon the joyous character of the celebration. This is reminiscent of Ezra 3:13 and 6:16.[216] On the other hand, there are great dissimilarities between this passage and previous sacrificial events. The listing of the participants and description of the procession make up almost the entire passage. The types or numbers of animals killed are not provided. The nature of the sacrificial ceremony is not described. The overall portrayal, however, is of a centralized

---

[215]The unity and extent of this source are difficult to ascertain. Certainly, most of Nehemiah 1-7 would be included. Also, large parts of 12:27-43 and 13:4-31 are composed of material from this source. For a detailed discussion of the Nehemiah Memoir, see Williamson, *Ezra-Nehemiah*, pp. xxiv-xxviii.

[216]Jacob M. Myers. *Ezra-Nehemiah*, AB (Garden City, New York, 1967), pp. 203-204. Myers argued that the five appearances in Nehemiah 12:43 of the root ח מ ש make joy the central element of the verse.

ceremony which brought together the entire community in the Jerusalem temple. There appears to have been no reason to provide graphic detail as in earlier accounts. The author had another agenda. The focus is on the importance of the wall, Nehemiah's great accomplishment. The covenant had been renewed in Jerusalem and the wall was around the city to protect and separate the community. The final act of Nehemiah, the expulsion of foreign wives in chapter 13, punctuated this expression of chosenness and security. With the fear and uncertainty of the early Restoration behind them, sacrifice became a formal, less urgent part of religious practice. Thus, from Ezra 7 through the end of Nehemiah, there is only this one relatively minor reference.

The Missing Sacrifice after
the Completion of the Wall

Given the pattern established in Chronicles and Ezra, as well as elsewhere in the Hebrew Bible, the reader would be likely to expect a sacrificial event immediately following the completion of the wall in Nehemiah. The absence of such a ceremony after Nehemiah 7:5 is something of a mystery. The immediate answer, of course, is that the Nehemiah Memoir was divided, placing the sacrificial event in chapter 12. Two difficult problems arise from this preliminary observation, however. First, why did the editor choose to arrange the material in this way? Second, what effect does this arrangement have on the meaning of the text? The answers to these two questions may be quite similar.

Williamson has suggested a compelling solution to the problem.[217]

---

[217]Williamson, *Ezra-Nehemiah*, p. 372. Williamson acknowledged that the dedication ceremony would have fit well after Nehemiah 7:3 or 6:19. Thus, it was moved thoughtfully. The parallels between the accounts of Ezra's activity in Nehemiah 8-10 and Nehemiah's activity in Nehemiah 11-12, along with their parallel portrayals in the procession in Nehemiah 12:31-39, are a further indication of an attempt to wed the reforms led by these two figures.

By inserting the covenant renewal, led by Ezra, between the completion of the wall and the account of the dedication ceremony and its sacrifices, the editor merged the physical building activities with the religious renewal. In Williamson's words, "The editor will not allow us to drive a wedge between religious and secular reform."[218] The effect of the movement of the ceremony is that it became the dedication of the entire restoration program, instead of simply the purification of a structure. Could it be that the finished wall provided the security that sacrificial ritual had provided earlier? This would explain a shift in emphasis removing the sense of urgency from sacrificial ritual. Was the Exile pushed far enough back into the editor's mind that the heightened focus it had created in the constructing of II Chronicles 29 - Ezra 6, had mostly evaporated?

---

[218]Ibid.

Chapter 4
THE SOCIAL FUNCTION OF SACRIFICE IN CHRONICLES, EZRA, AND NEHEMIAH

The importance placed on sacrificial ritual in Chronicles, Ezra, and Nehemiah, as illustrated in the previous two chapters, raises some additional questions. The writers of these books made extensive use of sacrificial events within the flow of their narratives. What does this emphasis say about the community which they have described in these texts which record the story of the Exilic period? What social function does sacrifice perform within the community implied by the text? Can analysis of these stories, in light of some modern ideas about sacrifice, reveal the social mechanisms operating within the narrative community? Are these social mechanisms compelling enough to account for the preoccupation with sacrificial ritual in the literature.

This chapter will begin with a background discussion of the socio-political situation in late sixth and early fifth century B.C.E. Palestine. This section is intended to provide a look at the range of possible conditions within which the returned community might have existed. This description should illustrate the potential problems that would be faced by a community recovering from exile, such as the community implied in the books of Chronicles, Ezra, and Nehemiah. Following this section, some modern understandings of the role of sacrifice in society and in literature will be presented. Finally, the discussion will return to the texts previously examined to ask how the sacrificial events described in the literature help this community handle its situation. The answer to this question is the aim of this chapter.[219]

An Overview of the
Socio-Political Situation
in Early Post-Exilic Palestine

Information related to the subject of this section has surfaced from time to time in the previous chapters of this study. There is tremendous uncertainty about conditions in Palestine during the late sixth and early fifth centuries. This is not intended as a comprehensive analysis of the subject, but a summary of some of the more important issues to serve as a backdrop for investigating the social function of sacrifice in the period. The topics surveyed will be the status of the province of Judah[220] in relation to the Babylonian empire, the social structure of the community, and the presence of group conflict in Palestine.

Conclusions about the political status of Judah during the first half century of the Restoration are closely tied to an understanding of the roles and positions of certain individual leaders. Exactly what sort of official position was held by Zerubbabel or Sheshbazzar is difficult to ascertain. Albrecht Alt put forth a very influential proposal that the Persians placed

---

[219]In an earlier article, "Sacrifice in II Chronicles 34-Ezra 6" (Presented at the Midwest Society of Biblical Literature at South Bend, Indiana, February 17, 1992), I examined the sacrificial texts in this smaller section in light of the theory of René Girard. The present chapter is an attempt to begin with a broader approach, using a number of perspectives on sacrifice.

[220]The term "Judah" is problematic. Some documents and artifacts from the era refer to a province called "Yehud." Seal impressions bearing this name appeared at the end of the fifth century B.C.E. See Ephraim Stern, "The Persian Empire and the Political and Social History of Palestine in the Persian Period," in *The Cambridge History of Judaism, Volume One: Introduction, the Persian Period*, ed. W. D. Davies and Louis Finkelstein (Cambridge: The Cambridge University Press, 1984), p. 83. The relationship between the two is uncertain. Exact geographic boundaries for the area before and after the Exile are not known. In this section "Judah" will simply refer to the region occupied by the returned community. Its political identity will be the subject of some of the discussion.

Judah under the control of the province of Samaria, and that this status was maintained until the appointment of Nehemiah as governor in 445.[221] More recently, Alt's position was confirmed by Sean E. McEvenue who systematically refuted a series of philologically based arguments that Judah had a greater status.[222] Alt's view was countered by Peter Ackroyd who contended that Zerubbabel and Sheshbazzar were governors of Judah.[223] Eric M. Meyers has taken a somewhat different position, that early post-Exilic Judah was independent while the appointment of Nehemiah as governor was an attempt by the Persians to exert greater control.[224] This dispute cannot be settled, of course. The incomplete nature of the records and the vagueness of terms are no more an argument for one side than the other. Ezra 1-6 presents a picture of the early returned community which appears to be a historical possibility. In their daily life these people were fairly autonomous. Nevertheless, there was significant turmoil in the area, and they were greatly dependent on Persian influence for security. Moreover, the Persian empire seems to have been quite capable of exerting such influence.

---

[221]Albrecht Alt, "Die Rolles Samarias bei der Entstehung des Judentums," in *Kleine Schriften zur Geschichte des Volkes Israel* (Munich: C. H. Beckische Verlagsbuchhandlung, 1953), pp. 331-332.

[222]Sean E. McEvenue, "The Political Structure in Judah from Cyrus to Nehemiah," *CBQ*, 43 (1981), 358-364. McEvenue demonstrated that the designation of Judah as מ ד י נ ה (province) in Ezra 2:1 and Nehemiah 7:6 is not conclusive evidence that it was an independent political entity, because this was a secondary classification of an area. The use of פ ח ה (governor) varies greatly in the book of Nehemiah and cannot be taken as a fixed official rank. McEvenue rejected the argument of Morton Smith (*Palestinian Parties and Politics that Shaped the Old Testament* [London: SCM Press, 1987], p. 149) that Judah had governors who ruled the area as an independent province prior to Nehemiah. Smith's position was primarily based on the ambiguous statement in Nehemiah 5:15. Finally, the title ה ת ר ש ת א, given to Zerubbabel in Ezra 2:63 and to Nehemiah in Nehemiah 8:9 and 10:2, varies too greatly in its meaning to give evidence of Judah's political status.

[223]Peter R. Ackroyd, "The Jewish Community in Palestine in the Persian Period," in *The Cambridge History of Judaism, Volume One: Introduction, The Persian Period*, ed. W. D. Davies and Louis Finkelstein (Cambridge: Cambridge University Press, 1984), pp. 155-156.

[224]Eric M. Meyers, "The Persian Period and the Judean Restoration from Zerubbabel to Nehemiah," in *Ancient Israelite Religion: Essays in Honor of Frank Moore Cross*, ed. Patrick D. Miller, et al. (Philadelphia: Fortress Press, 1987), pp. 516-517.

A thorough sociological analysis of early post-Exilic Israel is impossible. Researchers have not been able to come close to a consensus on even simple factual matters like the boundaries and population of the area. As mentioned earlier, population estimates have ranged from 10,000 to 235,000.[225] The level and type of social organization would certainly have depended upon the population density. A population at the lower end of the range mentioned above could have formed a relatively close-knit, cooperating community. On the other hand, the land might also have supported such a small number in a chaotic, subsistence type condition. Both of these would have been nearly impossible for a number in the hundreds of thousands, which would seem to have required wide dispersal, significant division of labor, and a developed infrastructure.

Most of the specific proposals concerning the structure of Judean society in the early post-Exilic period involve the operation of the Jerusalem temple as an economic center. A recent example of such a proposal is Joseph Blenkinsopp's "Civic-temple-community." This Persian sponsored program would have required two major accomplishments: 1) The seizing of land from the occupying peasantry, and 2) the building of the temple to serve as a "center of gravity for their existence."[226] The resulting conflict over land

---

[225]Tom E. Carter. "The Province of Yehud in the Persian Period: A Textual, Artifactual, and Geographic Approach" (Paper presented at The Society of Biblical Literature at Kansas City, Missouri, November 25, 1991), personal notes; and Edwin M. Yamauchi, "The Archaeological Background of Ezra," *BSac*, 137 (1980), 196-197. The lists presented in Ezra 2 and Nehemiah 7 would indicate an adult male population of about 25,000. See Richard A. Horsley, "Empire, Temple and Community--But Not Bourgeoise!: A Response to Blenkinsopp and Petersen," in *Second Temple Studies: 1. Persian Period*, ed. Philip R. Davies (Sheffield: Sheffield Academic Press, 1991), pp. 164-165. Horsley argued that this is a believable number for the whole of Judah, but not for the returnees alone.

[226]Joseph Blenkinsopp, "Temple and Society in Achaemenid Judah," in *Second Temple Studies: 1. Persian Period*, ed Philip R. Davies (Sheffield: Sheffield Academic Press, 1991), pp. 51-53. Blenkinsopp's proposal was a further development of J. Weinberg's *Burger-Tempel-Gemeinde* hypothesis ("Die Agrarverhältnisse in der Bürger-Tempel-Gemeinde der Achämenidzeit," in *Wirtschaft and Gesellschaft im Alten Vorderasien*, ed. J. Harmatta and G. Komoróczy [Tübingen: Mohr, 1976], pp. 473-486). Blenkinsopp contended that this was a standard Persian method of repatriating peoples. Richard A. Horsley ("Empire, Temple and Community . . . ") supported Blenkinsopp's premise, but stressed the Persian use of temples

created by this policy, or by other forces, will be discussed further below. Peter Ross Bedford countered Blenkinsopp, asserting that Jerusalem was not heavily populated until the time of Nehemiah, and that the temple did not control large amounts of land. These conditions would not have favored a temple dominated community.[227]

A very different proposal was offered by Heinz Kreissig. He concluded that the society of post-Exilic Judah was highly stratified along economic lines.[228] Kreissig identified three major strata present within the post-Exilic community - landowners, wage-earners, and slaves.[229] While conflict over land would indicate the development of stratification in a society, a highly developed system like Kreissig's would likely take considerable time to develop. Thus, it does not seem as applicable to the early years of the Restoration as to a later period in Judah.

The text of Ezra 1-6 indicates that the lives of the early returnees were centered about the temple to some degree, and that they saw the successful establishment of religious activity as essential to their total well-being. It is also obvious, however, that there were difficulties in gaining control over the land which the establishment of the temple did not solve easily. Even when

---

throughout the empire as a means of domination and exploitation. Paul D. Hanson ("Israelite Religion in the Early Post-Exilic Period," in *Ancient Israelite Religion*: Essays in Honor of Frank Moore Cross, ed. Patrick D. Miller, et al. [Philadelphia: Fortress Press, 1987], 493-501) used Frank Moore Cross's reconstruction of the textual history of Chronicles, Ezra, and Nehemiah. See Frank Moore Cross, "A Reconstruction of the Judean Restoration," (*JBL*, 94 [1975], 4-18) to illustrate a shift from hope in a Davidic leader to a Zadokite hierocracy, with political power placed in the hands of the political priesthood. In addition, Hanson argued that early post-Exilic prophetic texts, such as Haggai and Malachi, show a merging of prophetic and priestly concerns, with the economic prosperity of the land being closely linked to the successful operation of the temple (see Haggai 2:15-19).

[227]Peter Ross Bedford, "On Models and Texts: A Response to Blenkinsopp and Petersen," in *Second Temple Studies: 1. Persian Period*, ed. Philip R. Davies (Sheffield: Sheffield Academic Press, 1991), p. 159.

[228]Heinz Kreissig, *Die Sozialökonomische Situation in Juda zur Achämenidzeit* (Berlin: Akademie-Verlag, 1973), p. 115.

[229]Ibid., pp. 86-100.

some sense of control was accomplished, it was by the influence of the Persian empire. It is likely that on a day-to-day basis there was still considerable resistance to such control, even after the completion of the temple.

The presence of resistance gives rise to one final issue in the attempt to understand something of the sociology of the early post-Exilic period. What types of group conflict existed? How might this conflict have affected the lives of the members of the restored community? There were two potential types of conflict during this period, that between groups within the Restoration community, and that between the Restoration community and outside groups.

The most obvious tension was between the returnees and those who had remained in the land. This conflict appears in the early chapters of the book of Ezra, but appears to have been settled by the completion of the temple in chapter six. The conflict in Ezra is presented as religious in nature, but political and economic conflict were also inevitable.[230] It is indisputable that the Babylonians deported a significant number of Judahites, and that these would have been members of the upper levels of society. It is also certain that a large population was left behind, and that this group would have filled the vacuum by seizing land and whatever political and religious power remained in a seriously disrupted society. The return of those who had been deported was sure to have created a highly volatile social climate in post-Exilic Judah.

The assessment of conflict is complicated by additional issues, such as the highly debated origin of the Samaritans. As mentioned earlier, some interpreters see the conflict in Ezra 4:1-3 as at least one element in the

---

[230]See Carl Schultz, "The Political Tensions Reflected in Ezra-Nehemiah," in *Scripture and Context: Essays on the Comparative Method*, ed. Carl D. Evans, et al. (Pittsburgh: The Pickwick Press, 1980), p. 224. Schultz asserted that the conflict between the returnees and those who had remained in the land was essentially political and not religious.

process leading up to the Samaritan schism.[231] Little can be said with certainty about the ethnic relations of the early post-Exilic period. Again, the conflict which must have taken place was that over land and political power. To argue that religion and ethnicity had no part in it, however, is certainly an overstatement.[232]

The foregoing discussion indicates at least three major problems which may have existed in the Israelite community after the Exile: political instability, economic hardship, and group conflict. It is likely that these problems had often existed before the Exile, to a greater or lesser extent. In this situation of turmoil from a variety of sources, certain forces acted within the social matrix to create a somewhat unified community. In the following section it is argued that sacrificial ritual acts as one of these forces for the implied community of Chronicles, Ezra, and Nehemiah. Therefore, certain theories and ideas concerning the function of sacrifice will be examined in relation to the story of Exile and Restoration presented in Chronicles, Ezra, and Nehemiah to see what role it may have had in the social development of the community.

---

[231]See Wayne A. Brindle, "The Origin and History of the Samaritans," *GTJ* 5, (1984), 49-75. Brindle portrayed the Samaritan schism as a process covering six centuries. The exclusion in Ezra 4 was one step in the middle of this process. Those who connect Ezra 4:1-3 with Haggai 2:10-14, following J. W. Rothstein (*Juden und Samaritaner: Die Grundlegende Scheidung von Judentum und Heidentum* [Leipzig: J. C. Heinrichs, 1908], pp. 40-41), point to this religious conflict as the origin of the schism.

[232]There must have been conflict over the priesthood between the priests among the returnees and those who had assumed authority in Jerusalem during the Exile. A detailed description of one possible scenario is contained in the work of Hanson (*The People Called* [New York: Harper & Row, 1986], pp. 253-277; and *The Dawn of Apocalyptic* [Philadelphia: Fortress, 1975], pp. 32-269). Morton Smith (*Palestinian Parties and Politics that Shaped the Old Testament* [London: SCM Press, 1987], p. 62) highlighted the role of the "Yahweh-Alone Party" which returned to Palestine with the support of the Persian government to gain control of the land through the exercise of a politic-religioustemple hierocracy. For an example of how the analysis of religious conflict can be pushed too far see H. D. Mantel, "The Dichotomy of Judaism during the Second Temple," *Annual of the Hebrew Union College*, 44 (1973), 84-86. Mantel traced conflict between the sons of the *Golah* and the Zadokite high-priests all the way through to the first century C.E. conflict between the Sadducees and Pharisees.

Theories of Sacrifice

A tremendous amount of material has developed during the last century or so concerning the nature and role of sacrificial ritual in society. The most important for this study are the social theories of Émile Durkheim, the literary criticism of René Girard, and the studies of sacrifice in Semitic cultures by William Robertson Smith. The work of these authors will be summarized below. A section will also be included which surveys some of the more important contributions of biblical scholars to the understanding of sacrifice.

Émile Durkheim was perhaps the premier sociologist of the early twentieth century. In 1912 he published *Les Formes élémentaires de la vie religieux: Le système totemique en Australia*. This work was translated into English in 1915 as *The Elementary Forms of Religious Life: A Study in Religious Sociology*. In it Durkheim made some important observations about the function of sacrifice, based primarily on studies of central Australian tribes by Spencer, Gillen, Schulze, and Strehlowe.

The foundation of Durkheim's understanding of sacrifice was totemism, the representation of an individual or group by a specific type of animal or plant. By sacrificing and eating the totem an individual could "mark his place in society."[233] Durkheim carried the social function of sacrifice much farther, however. The ritual could also be used to assemble the group and strengthen their relations with each other. According to Durkheim, these social relations are "constantly combated and held in check by the antagonistic tendencies aroused and supported by the necessities of the daily

---

[233]Émile Durkheim, *The Elementary Forms of Religious Life: A Study in Religious Sociology*, trans. Joseph Ward Swain (London: George Allen & Unwin, Ltd., 1915), pp. 336-338. In this understanding, Durkheim adhered, at least in part, to W. Roberston Smith's view that the essence of sacrifice was a communal meal, not merely an act of renouncement. See later section on Smith.

struggle. "[234]   The individual is brought back into the group during a cooperative act, "For the spark of a social being which bears within him necessarily participates in this collective renovation."[235] Durkheim's social understanding of what may appear to be an individualistic religious ritual was also able to account for the periodicity of religious festivals. "...The rhythm which the religious life follows only expresses the rhythm of the social life, and results from it. Society is able to revivify the sentiment it has of itself only by assembling."[236] Thus, the social life is a cycle of dispersion and reconstitution. Sacrificial ritual serves as the focal element of reconstitution. Durkheim did not really address the question of why sacrifice, specifically, is so effective at serving this purpose.

William Robertson Smith is best known for his late nineteenth century work, *Lectures on the Religion of the Semites: The Fundamental Institutions*. While his end goal appears to have been the understanding of Israelite religion, as presented in the Hebrew Bible, his observations concerning sacrifice among Semitic peoples have had great influence on the study of sacrifice in general, as well as on biblical scholars.

Most notable among Smith's conclusions was his refutation of the prevailing gift-theory of sacrifice, as formulated by Herbert Spencer and Edward B. Tylor. He contended, on the contrary, that the origin of sacrifice was the act of communion.[237] The role of sacrifice deteriorated as less of the animal was eaten and more of it burned. The first step was the pouring out of the blood on the altar, followed by the burning of the fat portions (usually the kidneys and visceral organs). The final step away from the

---

[234]Ibid., p. 348.

[235]Ibid., p. 349.

[236]Ibid.

[237]William Robertson Smith, *Lectures on the Religion of the Semites: The Fundamental Institutions* (New York: Ktav, 1969), pp. 226-227.

communion meal was the development of the whole burnt offering. The tendency in this progression was a change from the idea of communion to a sin-offering.[238]

The earlier communion function of sacrifice had a clear social aspect, according to Smith. The renewal of the individual's bonds with God brought about a renewal of social bonds among people.[239] "The conception of man's chief good set forth in the social act of sacrificial worship is the happiness of the individual in the happiness of the community . . . ."[240] The sacrificial meal eaten with the deity created unity within society.[241]

Of all the writers who have theorized about the function of sacrifice, it is probably René Girard who is the most difficult to characterize, and who has been most influential in the past two decades. Part of the difficulty is categorizing Girard and his work. At heart he is a literary critic. He has approached the Bible only in its final form in French as a literary critic as well, never claiming any expertise in biblical scholarship. His work on sacrifice has based in literary study, though he does make frequent reference to the field-work of anthropologists such as Victor Turner, E. E. Evans-Pritchard, and Godfrey Lienhardt. Therefore, his work is very valuable in understanding literary texts such as those examined here in Chronicles, Ezra, and Nehemiah. Two works of Girard are central to this discussion, *La violence et le sacra*, published in 1972 and *Des choses cachées depuis la fondation du monde*, published in 1978.

Girard's theory of sacrifice may be summed up fairly simply. A society attempts to deflect the violence of its members onto a unanimous, innocent victim, thus maintaining stability among its members. This is an

---

[238]Ibid., pp. 346-352.

[239]Ibid., p. 263.

[240]Ibid., p. 267.

[241]Ibid., p. 269.

oversimplification, however.[242] There is an additional concept within Girard's work which must be considered, the somewhat slippery notions of "mimesis." This is the tendency of human beings to imitate one another. Mimesis leads to conflict because the imitator eventually desires the same object as the model.[243] Mimetic desire leads toward potential violence, what Girard calls "the sacrificial crisis." The function of sacrifice is to channel this conflict onto a third party, an innocent victim.[244] Sacrifice develops into a ritual pattern when this solution is repeated. The purpose of sacrificial ritual is "to reproduce . . . the miraculous event that put an end to the crisis, to immolate new victims substituted for the original victim in circumstances as close as possible to the original experience."[245]

Girard has identified the Bible as a book rooted in the sacrificial crisis.[246] This fits with his overall view of religion as a structure designed to "prevent the recurrence of reciprocal violence."[247] Because religion serves as the stabilizing force against violent breakdown, the decay of religious traditions poses a violent threat to society. It threatens the physical and spiritual foundation of the social group.[248]

---

[242]For Girard's summary of his own theory, see *Violence and the Sacred*, trans. Patrick Gregory (Baltimore: Johns Hopkins University Press, 1977), p. 8. For an example of this kind of over-simplification, and resulting dismissal see Jacob Milgrom, *Leviticus 1-16*, AB, vol. 3 (New York Doubleday & Co., 1991), p. 442.

[243]Girard, *Violence and the Sacred*, pp. 145-147.

[244]Ibid., pp. 78-79.

[245]René Girard, *Things Hidden Since the Foundation of the World*, trans. Stephen Bann and Michael Metteer (Stanford, California: Stanford University Press, 1987), pp. 20-21.

[246]Girard, *Violence and the Sacred*, p. 66.

[247]Ibid., p. 55.

[248]Ibid., p. 49. See also Girard, *Things Hidden*, p. 157. According to Girard, the progression of biblical history reveals that "mimetic and reciprocal violence is festering more and more as the old cultural forms tend to dissolve."

Biblical Scholars on Sacrifice

There are a number of biblical scholars whose names are readily identifiable with the subject of sacrifice, including Roland DeVaux, Jacob Milgrom, George Buchanan Gray, and W. O. E. Oesterley. Many others, of course, have also made important contributions to the understanding of sacrifice. Too often, however, the focus of study on this subject has been philological and theological. The assumption seems to have been that if one could only understand how and why particular terms are used in certain biblical passages, then one might ascertain the author's understanding of sacrifice, and the role that it played in Israel's religion. This creates two deficiencies in the study of biblical sacrifice. First, legal codes tend to receive far more attention than narrative descriptions of sacrificial events, because the former are rich with terminology. Therefore, understandings of post-Exilic sacrifice have typically been derived from Leviticus and Ezekiel 40-48, while the great sacrificial events in the Chronistic material have been all but ignored.[249] Second, the focus on legal material has created an emphasis on theological conclusions. On the other hand, sociological insights, which might be more easily obtained from examining events, are much less common.[250]

Gray and Oesterley both wrote comprehensive works on sacrifice during the first half of the twentieth century. Gray's approach was topical, including examinations of sacrifice in relation to the altar, the priesthood, and religious festivals. His explanations placed heavy emphasis on philology, and

---

[249]For instance, see George Buchanan Gray, *Sacrifice in the Old Testament: Its Theory and Practice* (New York: The Macmillan Company, 1925), pp. 427-430. Gray makes 181 references to Leviticus, but only eighty-nine to all of Chronicles, Ezra, and Nehemiah combined, with almost no substantive discussion of the events found in the latter.

[250]None of this is intended to imply that theological conclusions are unimportant, or that they cannot also be derived from studying narrative events, or even that legal material cannot help to inform sociological insights.

he tended to lean toward the gift theory as an overall perspective.[251] Most importantly, Gray attempted to demonstrate a change in the understanding of sacrifice in Israel at the time of the Exile. Pre-Exilic sacrifice was most often eucharistic in nature, while expiation became the dominant theme in post-Exilic times.[252] Oesterley's approach centered even more on historical development. He arrived at the conclusion, much like Gray, that post-Exilic sacrifice was primarily for the purpose of atonement.[253] The goal of sacrifice was the substitution of the life of the victim for the life of the sinner.[254]

A more recent, comprehensive treatment of biblical sacrifice appeared in the 1950's and 1960's in the work of Roland DeVaux. DeVaux's understanding of post-Exilic sacrifice continued along the lines of Gray and Oesterley. He admitted, however, that the focus on expiation in Ezekiel meant that it must have been a pre-Exilic idea. Nevertheless, he asserted that expiatory sacrifices were " . . . derivative forms, which assumed a greater importance when the great national calamities had given to the people a livelier sense of their culpability . . . ."[255]

Paul Hanson has outlined an understanding of the development of sacrifice as a practice emerging from an Exilic consciousness of sin. Werner H. Schmidt has proposed a further development of sacrificial practice in which

---

[251]Ibid., p. 2.

[252]Ibid., p. 95. Gray's focus on expiation in the post-Exilic period appears to be based largely on the frequency of sin and guilt offerings in the book of Ezekiel (p. 66). Note his fifty-two references to Ezekiel 40-48 alone (pp. 430-431).

[253]W. O. E. Oesterley. *Sacrifices in Ancient Israel: Their Origin, Purposes, and Development* (New York: The Macmillan Company, 1937), pp. 219-221. Oesterley also derived his position on post-Exilic sacrifice almost exclusively from Ezekiel.

[254]Ibid., p. 225. For this understanding, Leviticus 17:2 was Oesterley's basic text.

[255]Roland DeVaux, *Studies in Old Testament Sacrifice* (Cardiff: University of Wales Press, 1964), p. 106. DeVaux also argued that it would have been odd if entirely new cultic forms developed during the Exile when no cult was practiced (p. 103)

the words of praise offered during the sacrificial ritual were separated from the act and became independent. The words thus become a spiritualized form of sacrifice with a victim no longer utilized.[256]

Most recently, a thorough treatment of the subject of sacrifice has appeared in the work of Jacob Milgrom. Milgrom has taken some steps toward an understanding of the social function of sacrifice. In his interpretation of Leviticus 17:11, for example, sacrifice is the only proper way to slaughter an animal. Any other killing of an animal is murder.[257] In the final analysis, however, Milgrom has chosen to focus almost exclusively on the theological meaning of sacrificial ritual. The only purpose of sacrifice in the Bible is, he declared, "to induce the aid of the deity by means of a gift."[258]

Some biblical scholars have chosen to focus on the social function of sacrifice. J. H. M. Beattie has acknowledged this aspect in his overview of the subject, asserting that "Usually people sacrifice at times of personal or group crisis, or periodically...for the general good. Sacrifice serves some purpose for a group beyond just the affecting of forgiveness of sins.[259]

Ronald S. Hendel has gone a step further in his analysis of Exodus 24:3-8. While Exodus 24:24 explains sacrifice as a method of obtaining the favor of Yahweh, Hendel pointed to an additional function in his explanation

---

[256]Werner H. Schmidt, *The Faith of the Old Testament* (Philadelphia: Westminster Press, 1983), p. 132. Schmidt did admit that these types of expressions, found in the Psalms, may or may not have represented an actuality within cultic practice.

[257]Jacob Milgrom, "A Prolegomenon to Leviticus 17:11," *JBL*, 90 (1971), 152-155. In this analysis, Milgrom approaches Burkert's understanding of the hunt and its development into a sacrificial ritual in order to escape the guilt of killing. See Burkert, *Homo Necans*, pp. 20-22. Milgrom has acknowledged his agreement with Burkert's theory. See Milgrom, *Leviticus 1-11*, p. 442. This position is also confirmed by William H. Hallo. See William H. Hallo, "The Origins of the Sacrificial Cult: New Evidence from Mesopotamia and Israel," in *Ancient Israelite Religion: Essays in Honor of Frank Moore Cross*, ed. Patrick Miller, et al. (Philadelphia: Fortress Press, 1987), pp. 4-5.

[258]Milgrom, *Leviticus 1-11*, pp. 440-441.

[259]J. H. M. Beattie, "On Understanding Sacrifice," in *Sacrifice*, ed. M. E. C. Bourdillon and Meyer Fortes (New York: Academic Press, 1980), p. 32.

of the meaning of a pilgrimage festival. The pilgrimage is an enacted reunification of society.[260] Sacrifice operates as a very powerful set of symbols within the festival. The blood which is splashed on the altar, for example, remains there as a visual symbol, just as the blood on the doorposts in the original Passover.[261] This might help to explain why the blood was not consumed or burned with other parts of the victim. The blood splashed on the people also served as a ceremonial bonding between the members of the group.[262] Even the various methods of cooking the animals may have served as cultural symbols. According to Hendel, roasted meat, left partially raw, represented foreign or natural life. Boiled meat represented culture. Thus, boiled meat was typically eaten at festivals, but roasted meat could be eaten at Passover as a symbol of a foreign, detested life. On the other hand, meat offered to God was completely burned, or overcooked, representing God's position beyond culture.[263]

Finally, Gary A. Anderson has observed the combined religious and political meanings of sacrifices and offerings. The מ נ ח, for example, refers to both a cultic offering and a tax or tribute paid to governmental authorities.[264] The שׁ ל מ י ם (peace-offering) was used during the tribal period both to rally the troops together for battle and to celebrate victory. So powerful was the impact of this ceremony that I Samuel 13:9, II Samuel 6:17, and I Kings 9:25 record the efforts of Saul, David, and Solomon, respectively,

---

[260]Ronald S. Hendel, "Sacrifice as a Cultural Symbol: The Ritual Symbolism of Exodus 24:3-8," *ZAW*, 101 (1989), 371-377.

[261]Ibid., 387.

[262]Ibid., 388.

[263]Ibid., 383-387.

[264]Gary A. Anderson, *Sacrifices and Offerings in Ancient Israel: Studies in Their Social and Political Importance* (Atlanta: Scholars Press, 1987), p. 54.

to gain control over it.[265] Such use of sacrificial ceremonies makes it clear that sacrifice served far more than just an individual or corporate religious function.

With the preceding foundation laid, what conclusions are possible concerning the social function of sacrifice in the narrative accounts of Chronicles, Ezra, and Nehemiah? The review of the sociology of the Restoration period at the beginning of this chapter presented a portrait of a group of people struggling against both internal and external conflict to establish a stable community. The story of this community, and the experiences of their ancestors just before the Exile, found in Chronicles, Ezra, and Nehemiah indicates that sacrificial ritual may have played a central role its development. The preceding discussion of some recent views on sacrifice may offer some possible explanations as to why sacrificial ritual so preoccupies this portion of the Chronistic material. Can this literature, examined in light of these explanations, reveal the role of sacrifice in the community it describes? In order to answer this more general question, three specific questions may be asked of each of the sacrificial events considered in this study. What was the condition of the community when the event took place? What was the nature of the sacrificial ritual performed? What was the condition of the community after the ritual was completed?

The argument can be made that the biblical record gives only a narrative interpretation of the event, not an objective report. While this is true, it must not be allowed to prevent the use of such reports, which are the only available record. The results of such an inquiry must, however, be understood as applying only to the community in the narrative, due to this characteristic of the texts.

---

[265]Ibid., pp. 49-50.

II Chronicles 7:1-10

The initial dedication of Solomon's temple is the one event discussed in this study which appears to have taken place at a time of relative stability. This condition, however, should not be overstated. It is apparent from other texts, such as I Kings 12:4, that Solomon's support was not unanimous. Chronicles tends to avoid any negative reference to Solomon. Surely, some of the burden which the people experienced under Solomon's reign involved the building of the temple. The citizenry must have shared in the labor and the cost. Regardless of how the numbers of the sacrifices may have been exaggerated in the text, Solomon's generosity is highly visible in the story. The Chronicler chose to highlight this positive aspect of Solomon's actions. The people enjoyed twenty-three days of feasting at the expense of the government. The result of the prolonged, festive ceremony was that in II Chronicles 7:10 the people left "joyful and good of heart." For the Chronicler, this was a golden age moment. All was idyllic as a unified Israel worshipped in a properly dedicated temple. Any animosity toward Solomon is non- existent in the implied community of Chronicles. This is a clear indication of the unifying power of sacrificial ritual, as described by Durkheim and Robertson Smith, among others.[266]

II Chronicles 29:20-36

By the time of Hezekiah's reform, conditions were understood to have deteriorated badly from the glory days of Solomon. The people were not unified in worship, and the nation was at the threshold of crisis. The massive, unified sacrificial event recorded in these verses reflects the temple dedication of Solomon. The need for purification of the temple under Hezekiah

---

[266]See Durkheim, *The Elementary Forms*, p. 349, and Smith *Lectures*, p. 269.

indicates that religious divisions existed. Thus, the situation presented in Chronicles is one in which internal conflict can be assumed to be significant. In addition, the nation is experiencing the impending threat of Assyria to the north, which would culminate in Sennacherib's invasion in II Chronicles 32. The need to settle internal conflict in order to deal with this external enemy is great. In such a case, the effect of sacrificial ritual may be much more powerful than just a unifying, common meal.[267] The ability of the sacrificial act to deflect animosity and potential violence onto an innocent victim, as proposed by Evans-Pritchard, Lienhardt, and Girard, is operating in this narrative.[268] The violent threat posed by the deterioration of religious traditions is halted by a massive, unifying reform movement, which centers on sacrifice.

---

[267]The unifying meal is an important component of the influential theories of Herbert Spencer and Edward B. Tylor. For a presentation of this idea see Spencer, *The Principles of Sociology*, 3rd ed. (New York: D. Appleton and Company, 1896), pp. 99-106. Spencer traced the origin of religious sacrifices to funerary practices of leaving food for the deceased at the grave site. This type of ceremony easily developed into the giving of a gift of food to the deity (pp. 261-272). Though not speaking specifically of sacrifice, Spencer paralleled the social effect of funerary ritual and religious ritual. In the former, the gathering of family members in veneration of the dead often brought about the suspension of animosities within the family (pp. 95-98). In the latter, common religious festivals could bring about the cessation of hostilities between clans. Social unity could thus be created by common religious rituals (pp. 99-106).

[268]Girard, *Violence and the Sacred*, pp. 78-79. See also E. E. Evans-Pritchard, *Nuer Religion* (Oxford: The Clarendon Press, 1956), pp. 199-219. Evans-Pritchard commented that "...the sacrifices performed as a part of social activities are concerned with relations in the social order and not with relations between men and their natural environment." He described a sacrificial ceremony performed in order to settle a feud. In this ceremony the members of the groups pounced on the victim with tremendous fury, each hacking off whatever parts of the animal they could take hold of. Finally, Evans-Pritchard described the use of a clan spear name in a sacrificial ritual. The officiant would shout out the spear name during the immolation. The result of this practice was that "The sacrificial spear in his hand becomes through the exordium the clan sacrificial spear through which in symbol the whole clan offers up the victim to God." See also Godfrey Lienhardt, *Divinity and Experience: The Religion of the Dinka* (Oxford: The Clarendon Press, 1961), pp. 286-297. The most important sacrificial ritual which Lienhardt documented a sacrificial ritual performed by the Dinka tribe which was performed to settle a dispute between two parties. The animal victim was split in two as a visual symbol of the breaking of the feud relationship. The hostility of the two parties was enacted ceremonially upon the sacrificial victim. The death of the victim thereby became a source of life. In Lienhardt's words, "A Dinka sacrifice is in part, therefore, a drama of human survival." The violence that could have damaged the community found an outlet in the performance of sacrificial ritual.

II Chronicles 30:1-27

In one sense, the story of Hezekiah's Passover is just a continuation of the previous reform movement. There are some unique elements, however, which might reveal more clearly the role sacrifice is playing in the community in this narrative. The most outstanding feature of the ceremony is the tremendous effort Hezekiah makes to include the Northern Kingdom. The shared festival may serve to bring about the settling of differences between the two kingdoms, to at least some degree. The relationship between the two kingdoms in conflict may approach Girard's concept of mimesis.[269] Are the two nations in the Chronicler's narrative competing to be the chosen people, both desiring a common object - the true religious heritage of ancient Israel?[270] If so, then the Passover festival provides an outlet for settling the resulting sacrificial crisis, even if the effect is not thorough or long-lasting.

II Chronicles 34:1-7

The ascension of Josiah finds Judah once again in religious disarray. The Chronicler's account, at this point, is rapidly accelerating toward destruction. Internal conflict is again matched by external threat, this time the northward advance of the Egyptian army under Neco. The first recorded act of Josiah within this context is the purifying of worship by the destruction of the high places. Unlike the other sacrificial events in II Chronicles, this is not a large-scale festival involving the massive slaughtering of animals. Instead, this act produces the necessary purification leading up to the festive scene in II Chronicles 35. In one sense, the human sacrifices at the high places make

---

[269]Girard, *Violence and the Sacred*, pp. 145-147.

[270]The Syro-Ephraimitic War of the late eighth century provides one example of direct, violent conflict between Judah and Israel.

possible the resolution of conflict in Judah. In another sense, however, this
is a very non-sacrificial act. The unity and deflection of violence which might
be produced by a sacrificial ritual does not occur before the spilling over of
violent passions. The conflict, in part, is settled when one of the parties
slaughters the other. Nevertheless, it is important to note that only the
leaders of those who worshipped away from the temple are killed, while the
masses are later unified in a common festival. Thus, in the final analysis, the
killing of the priests performs a sacrificial function.

II Chronicles 35:1-19

Josiah's Passover is Judah's last stand against a tidal wave of chaos and
destruction; though the outcome is already decided, as the Chronicler
indicates in 34:28.[271] Along with Hezekiah's Passover, this great religious
festival illustrates the socio-religious cycle of dispersion and reconstitution, as
outlined by Durkheim.[272] In both cases, sacrifice functioned as the focal
element of reconstitution. As in Hezekiah's Passover, traditions of the
festival were blended in order to place priority on unity. Societal and
religious disarray becomes order in the unifying festival.

II Chronicles 36:15-21

Like the reform of Josiah, the horrifying destruction of Jerusalem
serves partly as an example of the failure of sacrifice. The telescoped
portrayal of the last kings of Judah in 36:1-14 is the epitome of internal
conflict and confusion. The alternating alliances with and rebellions against

---

[271]Hendel's assertion that roasted meat consumed at Passover celebrations served as a
symbol of a foreign, abominable life may be relevant here. See Hendel, "Sacrifice as a Cultural
System," 383-387. It is only in Josiah's Passover that roasting is specifically mentioned.

[272]Durkheim, *The Elementary Forms*, p. 349.

foreign powers, Egypt and Babylon, indicate a clearly divided nation in political turmoil. Previous movements to unify the nation had waned in their influence, and no reformer of the likes of Hezekiah and Josiah steps forward to halt the downhill slide. The threat of religious decay, as proposed by Girard, becomes more than a threat in this chapter.[273] While the destruction of Jerusalem is a devastating, negative event, it also paves the way for a new beginning. A hint at this new start appears in the final verses of Chronicles, the decree of Cyrus. This possibility would begin its fulfillment in the early years of the Restoration, when sacrifice once again surfaces as the central concern of the reconstituted community in the narrative of Ezra.

Ezra 3:1-6, 4:1-5

The first recorded act of the returnees in the narrative of Ezra is the setting up of the altar in order to offer sacrifices. Once again, a time of crisis is at hand. Ezra 3:3 indicates that the returned community is in fear of the surrounding peoples. The acts of sacrifice in 3:4-6 may serve two purposes. First, a community ritual performs precisely the function that Robertson Smith proposed. The renewal of relations with God creates a renewal of social relations between the individuals of the community.[274] Second, even though the temple is not yet rebuilt, a link is forged between the stabilizing religious institutions of the past and the present situation. The new altar, resting on a site purified by the blood of innocent young Israelites, becomes the central unifying symbol for the fragile new community.

The approach and rejection of the other group in Ezra 4:1-5 brings about mimetic conflict, both parties believing themselves to be the possessor

---

[273]Girard, *Violence and the Sacred*, p. 47. Of course Israel was destroyed by a powerful enemy, but the picture painted in II Chronicles 36 portrays a nation ripe for destruction, and not likely to withstand any type of invasion.

[274]Smith, *Lectures*, p. 263.

of Israel's religious tradition. This conflict postpones the building of the new temple, halting the progress of reorganizing the community. Throughout the book of Ezra, sacrificial ceremonies serve to define and redefine the community.

Ezra 6:16-18

The next time the community acts in Ezra's narrative is when the temple is finished and dedicated. The most important social aspect of the dedication of the new temple is probably the link it forms with the traditions of the past, especially Solomon's dedication. The sacrificial ritual once again reconstitutes the community around a central shrine. That these verses appear in Aramaic is tremendously important for understanding how they fit into this interpretation of the narrative. This temple dedication brings to an end the conflict and crisis which had arisen between the two groups during the events recorded at the beginning of Ezra 4. These verses go with the material that appears before them more than that which comes after them.[275] They form the resolution to the earlier narrative.

Ezra 6:19-22

The Passover recorded here in Ezra illustrates an important social shift. The sacrificial ritual serves as an important act of inclusion as well as exclusion. Ezra 6:21 indicates that others are brought into the community at

---

[275]See Walter Burkert, *Homo Necans: The Anthropology of Ancient Greek Sacrificial Ritual and Myth*, trans. Peter Bing (Berkeley: University of California Press, 1983), pp. 38-40. Burkert's observations about the life-giving power of a sacrifice offered for a structure may be very relevant here. According to Burkert, The power of sacrifice lies in the experience of death. He attempted to explain how this power could continue to operate in less primitive situations. The person or object for which the sacrifice is made is exposed to "the abyss of annihilation." It has essentially passed through death. Thus, for example, a building for which sacrifice is offered is transformed and given enduring power.

this point. That their entry into the community is signaled by a sacrificial event is no accident.[276] Though the details are not mentioned specifically, the Passover celebration would have involved the splashing of the lamb's blood on the altar and on the people. Hendel has emphasized the importance of these two symbols, the first being a lasting visual image, and the second a symbolic bonding of the members of the group.[277] The latter symbol would have been especially important at an occasion where new members were incorporated into the community.

Ezra 8:35

Though outside the literary unit of Ezra 1-6, this brief sacrificial event further exemplifies the social function of sacrifice in the earlier narrative. The Ezra group comes to Jerusalem to join a community which had originated more than a half century earlier. Surely, this is no painless integration of two groups, one already established in the land, the other an elite band of interlopers with royal decree in hand. The potential for mimetic conflict between the two groups is great. Again, there is an urgent need to redefine the community. As before, this is accomplished by an act of sacrifice. By coming immediately to the temple, the center of existence for the Restoration

---

[276]See Edmund Leach, 'The Logic of Sacrifice," in *Anthropological Approaches to the Old Testament*, ed. Bernhard Lang (Philadelphia: Fortress Press, 1985), p. 156. An example of the use of a structural approach to sacrifice in the Bible is Leach's analysis of certain sacrificial rites in Leviticus, such as the reentering of society by a leper and the cleansing of an uninhabitable house. Because structuralism assumes a sense of rational order in human institutions, such rites cannot be accepted as mere superstitions. Leach established a continuum between the poles of sacred and profane. With the former he grouped God, temple, life, and order. With the latter he placed Gentiles, wilderness, death, and chaos. The function of the sacrificial rites was to return life situations back to the good side of the continuum. Leach concluded that 'Sacrifice has to do with the correction of social disruption and the reformation of confused categories." The community in Ezra seems highly conscious of insiders and outsiders. The joining of new individuals to the community requires just this type of correction of confused categories.

[277]Hendel, 'Sacrifice as a Cultural Symbol," 387-388.

104

community, and joining in a sacrificial ritual, the new group performs a powerful symbolic act of unification.[278]

The adding of new members to the Restoration community in Ezra may be viewed as part of a cyclical social process.[279] The sacrificial rituals performed on these occasions, both here in 8:35 and in Ezra 6:19-22, signal the end of a former community and the beginning of a new one. The individual purposes of the old community and the entering group die in the sacrificial ritual, giving birth to the future hopes of a newly constituted community.

Nehemiah 12:27-43

The most important social factor in this text is the explicit inclusion of the entire Restoration community. As a renewal ceremony, this is part of the normal religious cycle of dispersion and reconstitution.[280] In addition, this ceremony is organized and conducted by a highly visible, political leader. Anderson's description of the attempts of leaders, such as Saul and David, to

---

[278]As noted in the discussion of this passage in the previous chapter, the language of this text does not preclude participation in this event by members of the established community.

[279]See Victor Turner, *The Drums of Affliction: The Study of Religious Processes among the Ndembu of Zambia*, (Oxford: The Clarendon Press, 1968), p. 277. The presence of sacrifice in most rituals led Turner to focus on the process of victimization in society. This process is a two-edged sword, bringing suffering to some, but life to the community in crisis. Turner summed up his understanding of sacrifice in this concluding statement:

> Thus sacrifice, as representing the end of a cycle is "sacrifice" indeed, a death of many personal and sectional strivings and desires for the sake of social renewal. But sacrifice, as representing the beginning of a cycle, is also a birth and a hope for the future which will follow the same general course as the past.

The redefining of a community when it is joined by a new group would require this kind of change in purpose and identity.

[280]Durkheim, *The Elementary Forms*, p. 349

gain control of sacrifice is applicable here as well.[281] The event in Nehemiah 12 is no mere religious celebration involving a gift to the deity. Sacrificial ritual serves as a powerful social and political symbol which accomplishes the unification of the people under a defined hierarchy of leadership.

Summary

In the narrative leading up to the Exile and on through the Restoration, which is presented in II Chronicles, Ezra, and Nehemiah, all of the crucial, defining moments for the community are sacrificial rituals. While these sacrifices might be understood, at least in part, as gifts to God for the purpose of expiation and the granting of divine favor, they also play a role within the community portrayed in the narrative. These sacrificial ceremonies accomplish several social purposes: 1) They unify the community at times of internal conflict and external threat, 2) they define the community by establishing boundaries of inclusion and exclusion, 3) they provide an outlet for the potential violence of group conflict, and 4) they serve as a means for political leaders to consolidate and demonstrate their leadership. As this chapter has illustrated, these functions of sacrificial ritual become clear when the sacrificial events recorded in the biblical text are examined as social events. While terminology and background in the legal tradition are important, they are not used consistently in these portrayals, and do not appear to have been the primary concern of the authors. The central issue in these texts is the meaning of sacrificial ritual for the faith community portrayed in the narrative. The purposes of sacrifice listed above establish the necessity of sacrifice for the cohesiveness and viability of such a community.

---

[281]Anderson, *Sacrifices and Offerings in Ancient Israel*, p. 54.

Chapter 5

CONCLUSION

A complete picture of the actual history of Israel during the period around the Exile cannot be attained. The best evidence available concerning that time period is the written texts in the Bible. The only source for many of the events from the eighth to the fourth century is the literary history contained in the books of Chronicles, Ezra, and Nehemiah. In looking at these books, it becomes apparent that in recording the story of Israel just prior to, during, and immediately following the Exile, sacrifice was a major concern of the writers. It is not a tremendous leap to assume that what appears as the major concern of the writer in the text was also the major concern of the community.[282]

Summary

In Chapter Two the texts in II Chronicles describing sacrificial events were analyzed to determine their central focus and the role those events played in this literary account of the decline and fall of Judah. The reform movements and Passover celebrations of Hezekiah and Josiah perform two

---

[282]See Donn F. Morgan, *Between Text and Community: The "Writings" in Canonical Interpretation* (Minneapolis: Fortress Press, 1990), p. 66. Such an understanding of the function of the text is present in Morgan's assertion concerning Chronicles that "...this history is an interpretive lens through which we must look if we are to understand the pertinence and applicability of the past. More important, perhaps, 1-2 Chronicles represents paradigmatically a process, the rereading and reinterpretation of the story for present communities, in which all subsequent communities must engage."

major functions in the narrative. First, there is an intense concern in these texts for presenting massive sacrificial events in which all of Israel participates. Therefore, these sacrificial rituals act as unifying moments for the community during times of crisis. Second, these texts, along with the presentation of the destruction of Jerusalem in II Chronicles 36 as the sacrificing of Israel, stand as a sign to later communities that the clue to living successfully as God's people is the proper maintenance of the sacrificial cult. Though leadership roles may have been less defined in the post-Exilic period than in the monarchy, sacrificial ritual would always be an important tool in the hands of community leaders, especially in times of instability.[283]

Chapter Three demonstrated the continuing focus upon sacrifice in the first half of the book of Ezra, and the waning of its importance in the remainder of Ezra and Nehemiah. At crucial moments in the early development of the community described in Ezra, such as the initial return to the land, the dedication of the new temple, and the return of the group led by Ezra, sacrificial ritual always emerges as a mechanism for developing community. For example, an important tension between inclusion and exclusion is set up in Ezra 6:19-22. The sacrificial ritual of Passover is able to accomplish dual purposes, the incorporation of new members into the community and the defining of boundaries which keep others out.

In viewing Chronicles, Ezra, and Nehemiah together, it is important to notice the increase in concentration of sacrificial events heading into the Exile, and the decrease of attention to sacrifice as the community solidified

---

[283]It has been suggested that this connection of post-Exilic institutions to the great traditions of Israel's history is the primary function of Chronicles. See Sara Japhet, *The Ideology of the Book of Chronicles and Its Place in Biblical Thought* (Frankfurt: Verlag Peter Lang, 1989), p. 516. Japhet claimed the purpose of Chronicles was to bridge the gap of history created by the Exile by reformulating history so that traditions would become relevant to the present, yet would be given authority by their connection with the past. See also Rex Mason, *Preaching the Tradition: Homily and Hermeneutics after the Exile* (Cambridge: Cambridge University Press,1990), pp. 260-262. Mason observed that when a people's existence "can no longer be guaranteed in political terms, the continuity of the outward forms and institutions of their faith and their separated life as a community of that faith become all important."

after the exile. In addition, the existence of any kind of sacrificial ritual during the period of Exile is completely ignored. An overall picture emerges in which sacrifice is the dominant theme. What this portrait accomplishes is an understanding that sacrifice was the method of unifying community in the past, is the key to understanding the destruction and Exile of Judah, is the legacy of the returned community alone, and is the secret to ensuring prosperity in the future. The debate concerning the relationship of these books may never be settled conclusively, but this literary development may reveal a link between the works, at least in their final forms.[284]

Chapter Four was an attempt to understand the sociological function of sacrifice in the communities described in the narratives of Chronicles, Ezra and Nehemiah, as revealed by the texts examined in the second and third chapters. The survey of modern views of the social function of sacrifice produced helpful models which might be applied to events described in the biblical texts. The views of Durkheim, Robertson Smith, and Girard find remarkable confirmation in the behavior of the communuities portrayed in these stories.

The application of modern insights into the social function of sacrifice to the events depicted in Chronicles, Ezra, and Nehemiah exposes important social dimensions within these events which go far beyond a simple desire to bring about expiation of sin. The inclusion and exclusion of various groups within the ritual helps to establish and maintain the boundaries of the community. This is one reason why sacrificial rituals take place at times when new members are incorporated into the community, as in Ezra 6:19-22 and 8:35. The control of sacrificial ritual serves as an important occasion for political leaders to assert authority. This dimension is present in the reform ceremonies of Hezekiah and Josiah and the dedication and renewal ceremony

---

[284]See Joseph Blenkinsopp, *Ezra-Nehemiah*, OTL (Philadelphia: Westminster Press, 1988), p. 54. Blenkinsopp has demonstrated a progression of festival references in Chronicles and Ezra-Nehemiah which serve as a strong indication of a "unity of conception which binds together the two works into one history with its own distinctive point of view."

in Nehemiah 12. By conducting the rituals personally, these leaders create a visual symbol of their position in the community. Sacrifice also serves to relieve internal strife, unifying the community in times of crisis. This takes place in the reform movements of Hezekiah and Josiah, and after the initial return of some of the Exiles to Jerusalem in Ezra 3.

Many interpreters of Chronicles, Ezra, and Nehemiah have observed that the cult receives a tremendous amount of attention in these books, particularly the temple cult in Jerusalem. The realization that sacrificial ritual was such a vital social force in the post-Exilic community reveals why cultic matters received such emphasis. A centralized cult is the only place where sacrificial ritual can exert such powerful and commanding influence over an entire society. For sacrifice to play this kind of role on a national level, localized practice would have to be halted, or at least severely limited.

Possibilities for Further Research

The results of this study might be taken in several different directions. First, texts outside of the Chronistic material might be examined in a manner similar to the analysis in chapters two and three of this study. While large scale sacrificial events are not as prevalent in other portions of the Hebrew Bible, references to sacrifice are still quite frequent. A study of such references in the Psalms or the prophetic books might provide important information for understanding the role of sacrifice in various periods of Israelite society. The combination of texts from the whole of the Bible might reveal important historical developments in the use of sacrificial ritual.

Donn F. Morgan's understanding of how the post-Exilic community shaped the text of the Writings supports the idea that the Bible reveals much about the nature of the communities that produced it.[285]

---

[285]Morgan, *Between Text and Community*, p. 30. Morgan also assumed the reverse process. The text, Torah and Prophets, shaped the communities that produced the writings.

Second, the development of sacrifice through history after the immediate post-Exilic period needs to be analyzed in the same way. What is the understanding of sacrifice which might emerge from a study of apocryphal and pseudepigraphical literature? If such a development could be traced through the final centuries before the common era and on into the New Testament period, important insight into the understanding of the crucifixion in the gospels, and an epistle like Hebrews, might be gained. This possibility leads to the consideration of whether or not a comprehensive biblical theology of sacrifice might be developed.[286] Such a theology would need to take into account not only the religious aspects, but also the social and political dimensions of sacrificial ritual.

Third, any serious work dealing with Chronicles, Ezra, and Nehemiah must recognize the importance of these books for an understanding of the canon. What does the placement of these particular books in the Hebrew Canon, the Christian Canon, and the Septuagint mean? Can the proposal that sacrifice is the central concept, at least in the section from II Chronicles 29 - Ezra 6, help explain the placement and meaning of these books in relation to the rest of the Bible? Eric Gans has proposed that Chronicles is placed after Ezra and Nehemiah in the Hebrew Bible so that the second temple destruction (in 70 C. E.) would be assimilated into the first. The idea of restoration then "became a stable temporal horizon unrelated to concrete acts."[287] The rallying cry at the end of II Chronicles, "let him go up,"[288] may serve as a call to faithfulness in the face of despair and destruction in all

---

[286]An important step in this direction has appeared recently in the work of James G. Williams. Though his book deals specifically with the intersection of religion and violence, sacrifice may be understood as the most important component of that intersection. See James G. Williams, *The Bible, Violence, and the Sacred* (San Francisco: HarperSanFrancisco, 1991).

[287]Eric Gans, *The End of Culture*: Toward a Generative Anthropology (Berkeley: University of California Press, 1985), p. 207.

[288]Recall the proposal of Eskenazi that this final word could also be translated "let him sacrifice." See Tamara Cohn Eskenazi, "The Chronicler and the Composition of I Esdras," *CBQ*, 48 (1986), 57.

times, even today.

Finally, the study of religion appears to be making a start at understanding violence and its relationship to religion. The post-Exilic community should represent an important model for study. This model is particularly useful because a written legacy remains, a very extensive written legacy if the final form of the entire Hebrew Bible was influenced by this period. How does religion, highlighted by sacrificial ritual, interact with the violent tendencies of society. The Chronistic material indicates that sacrifice, a violent act in itself, may have served as a stabilizing influence in society. The vast majority of modern religions are devoid of any real sacrificial rituals. Are there other potentially stabilizing influences in modern religion? Some observers have proposed that the modern justice system has replaced the religious sacrificial system as the regulator of reciprocal violence.[289] Recent events in Los Angeles, however, have vividly portrayed the devastating results of the failure of this system. Perhaps, though the concept of blood sacrifice is no longer morally acceptable, it is time for religion to reexamine its role in society, with an understanding of the function of sacrificial ritual in the past, in order to develop new and creative ways of settling violent conflict.

---

[289]See Forrest Wood, "Averting Violence: Social and Personal," *Perspectives in Religious Studies*, 14 (1978), 31. Wood's conclusions are based on René Girard's writing on this idea. See René Girard, *Violence and the Sacred*, trans. Patrick Gregory (Baltimore: Johns Hopkins University Press, 1977), p. 18.

Table of Abbreviations

AB	Anchor Bible
BRev	*Bible Review*
BSac	*Bibliotheca Sacra*
CBQ	*Catholic Biblical Quarterly*
CHJ	*Cambridge History of Judaism*
CTM	*Concordia Theological Monthly*
GTJ	*Grace Theological Journal*
HJT	*The Heythrop Journal*
HTR	*Harvard Theological Review*
Interp	*Interpretation*
JBL	*Journal of Biblical Literature*
JNSL	*Journal of Northwest Semitic Languages*
JSS	*Journal of Semitic Studies*
JTS	*Journal of Theological Studies*
NCBC	New Century Bible Commentary
NICOT	New International Commentary on the Old Testament
OTL	Old Testament Library
PTR	*Princeton Theological Review*
TBT	*The Bible Today*
TCBC	The Cambridge Bible Commentary
TynB	*Tyndale Bulletin*
VF	*Verkündigung und Forschung*

VT	*Vetus Testamentum*
WBC	Word Biblical Commentary
ZAW	*Zeitschrift für die Altestamentliche Wissenschaft*

BIBLIOGRAPHY

Books

Ackroyd, Peter R. *The Chronicler in His Age*. Sheffield,England: Sheffield Academic Press, 1991.

_____. *Exile and Restoration*. Old Testament Library. Philadelphia: Westminster Press, 1968.

_____. "The Jewish Community in Palestine in the Persian Period." In *Introduction, the Persian Period*. Vol. 1 of *The Cambridge History of Judaism*. Ed. W. D. Davies and Louis Finkelstein. Cambridge: Cambridge University Press, 1984.

Albright, William F. *The Archaeology of Palestine*. Baltimore: Penguin Books, 1949.

Allen Leslie C. *The Translator's Craft*. Part 1 of *The Greek Chronicles: The Relation of the Septuagint of I and II Chronicles to the Masoretic Text*. Supplements to *Vetus Testamentum*, vol. 25. Leiden: E.J. Brill, 1974.

_____. *Textual Transmission*. Part 2 of *The Greek Chronicles: The Relation of the Septuagint of I and II Chronicles to the Masoretic Text*. Supplements to *Vetus Testamentum*, vol. 27. Leiden: E.J. Brill, 1974.

Alt, Albrecht. "Die Rolles Samarias bei der Entstehung des Judentums." In *Kleine Schriften zur Geschichte des Volkes Israel*. Munich: C. H. Beckische Verlagsbuchhundlung, 1953.

Anderson, Gary A. *Sacrifices and Offerings in Ancient Israel: Studies in Their Social and Political Importance*. Atlanta: Scholars Press, 1987.

Attridge, H. W. "Historiography." In *Jewish Writings of the Second Temple Period*. Philadelphia: Fortress Press, 1984.

Avi-Yonah, M. "The Walls of Nehemiah: A Minimalist View." In *Israel Exploration Journal Reader*, vol. 2. Ed. Harry M. Orlinsky. New York: Ktav Publishing House, 1981.

Beattie, J. H. M. "On Understanding Sacrifice." In *Sacrifice*. Ed. M. E. C. Bourdillon and Meyer Fortes. New York: Academic Press, 1980.

Bedford, Peter Ross. "On Models and Texts: A Response to Blenkinsopp and Peterson." In *Second Temple Studies: 1. Persian Period*. Ed. Philip R. Davies. Sheffield: Sheffield Academic Press, 1991.

Blenkinsopp, Joseph. *Ezra-Nehemiah*. Old Testament Library. Philadelphia: Westminster Press, 1988.

_____. "Temple and Society in Achaemenid Judah." In *Second Temple Studies: 1. Persian Period*. Ed. Philip R. Davies. Sheffield: Sheffield Academic Press, 1991.

Braun, Roddy L. *1 Chronicles*. Word Biblical Commentary, vol. 14. Waco, Texas: Word Publishing, 1986.

_____. "Chronicles, Ezra, and Nehemiah: Theology and Literary History. In Supplements to *Vetus Testamentum*, vol. 30. Leiden: E. J. Brill, 1979.

Budd, Philip J. "Holiness and Cult." *Ancient Israel: Social, Anthropological, and Politial Perspectives*. Ed. Ronald E. Clements. Cambridge: Cambridge University Press, 1989.

Burkert, Walter. *Homo Necans*: The Anthropology of Ancient Greek Sacrificial Ritual and Myth. Trans. Peter Bing. Berkeley: University of California Press, 1983.

Childs, Brevard. *Introduction to the Old Testament as Scripture*. Philadelphia: Fortress Press, 1979.

Clines, D. J. A. *Ezra, Nehemiah, Esther*. New Century Bible Commentary. Wm. B. Eerdmans Publishing Co., 1984.

Cogan, Mordechai. "The Chronicler's Use of Chronology as Illuminated by Neo-Assyrian Royal Inscriptions." In *Empirical Models for Biblical Criticism*. Ed. Jeffrey H. Tigay. Philadelphia: University of Pennsylvania Press, 1985.

Coggins R. J. *The Books of Ezra and Nehemiah*. The Cambridge Bible Commentary. Cambridge, England: Cambridge University Press, 1976.

_____. *The First and Second Books of Esdras.* The Cambridge Bible Commentary. Cambridge, England: Cambridge University Press, 1976.

_____. *Samaritans and Jews: The Origins of Samaritanis Reconsidered.* Atlanta: John Knox Press, 1975.

Cross, Frank M. *The Ancient Library at Qumran and Modern Biblical Studies.* Garden City, New York: Doubleday & Co., 1961.

Curtis, Edward Lewis and Albert Alonzo Madsen. *A Critical and Exegetical Commentary on the Books of Chronicles.* International Critical Commentary. New York: Charles Scribner's Sons, 1910.

Davies, Douglas. "An Interpretation of Sacrifice in Leviticus." In *Anthropological Approaches to the Old Testament.* Ed. Bernhard Lang. Philadelphia: Fortress Press, 1985.

LeDeaut, R. and J. Robert. *Introduction and Traduction.* Vol. 1 of *Targum des Chronique.* Rome: Biblical Institute Press, 1971.

_____. *Texte et Glassarie.* Vol. 2 of *Targum Des Chronique.* Rome: Biblical Institute Press, 1971.

DeVries, Simon J. *1 and 2 Chronicles.* Grand Rapids, Michigan: Wm. B. Eerdmans Publishing Company, 1989.

Dillard, Raymond B. *II Chronicles.* Word Biblical Commentary. Waco, Texas: Word Publishing, 1987.

Douglas, Mary. *Purity and Danger.* New York: ARK, 1966.

Driver, Samuel R. *An Introduction to the Literature of the Old Testament.* Edinburgh: T & T Clark, 1913.

Duke, Rodney K. *The Persusive Appeal of the Chronicler.* Sheffield, England: The Almond Press, 1990.

Durkheim, Émile. *The Elementary Forms of the Religious Life: A Study in Religious Sociology.* Trans. Joseph Ward Swain. London: George Allen & Unwin, Ltd., 1915.

Elmslie, W. A. L. "Ezra-Nehemiah." *Interpreter's Bible*, vol. 3. Ed. George Buttrick. Nashville: Abingdon, 1954.

Eskenazi, Tamara Cohn. *In an Age of Prose: A Literary Approach to Ezra-*

Nehemiah. Atlanta: Scholars Press, 1988.

Evans-Pritchard, E. E. *Neur Religion.* Oxford: The Clarendon Press, 1956.

_____. *Theories of Primitive Religion.* Oxford: The Clarendon Press, 1965.

Fensham, F. Charles. *The Books of Ezra and Nehemiah.* New International Commentary on the Old Testament. Grand Rapids, Michigan: Wm. B. Eerdmans Publishing Co., 1982.

Frazer, James George. *The Golden Bough: A Study in Magic and Religion.* New York: The MacMillan Company, 1935.

Friedman, Richard Elliot. *The Exile and Biblical Narrative: The Formation of the Deuteronomistic and Priestly Works.* Chico, California: Scholars Press, 1981.

Galling, Kurt. *Die Bücher der Chronik, Esra, Nehemia.* Göttingen: Bandenhoeck & Ruprecht, 1954.

Gans, Eric. *The End of Culture: Toward a Generative Anthropology.* Berkeley: University of California Press, 1985.

Girard, René. *Things Hidden Since the Foundation of the World.* Trans. Stephen Bann and Michael Metteer. Stanford, California: Stanford University Press, 1987.

_____. *Violence and the Sacred.* Trans. Patrick Gregory. Baltimore: Johns Hopkins University Press, 1977.

Graham, Matthew Patrick. *The Utilization of 1 and 2 Chronicles in the Reconstruction of Israelite History in the Nineteenth Century.* Atlanta: Scholars Press, 1990.

Gray, George Buchanan. *Sacrifice in the Old Testament: Its Theory and Practice.* Oxford: The Clarendon Press, 1925.

Hallo, William H. "The Origins of the Sacrificial Cult: New Evidence from Mesopatamia and Israel." In *Ancient Israelite Religion: Essays in Honor of Frank Moore Cross.* Ed. Patrick D. Miller, et al. Philadelphia: Fortress Press, 1987.

Halpern, Baruch. "A Historiographic Commentary on Ezra 1-6: A Chronological Narrative and Dual Chronology in Israelite History." In *The Hebrew Bible and Its Interpreters.* Ed. William Henry Propp, et

118

al. Winona Lake, Indiana: Eisenbrauns, 1990.

Hamerton-Kelly, Robert G., ed. *Violent Origins: Ritual Killing and Cultural Formation.* Stanford, California: Stanford University Press, 1987.

Hammerschaimb, E. *Some Aspects of OT Prophecy from Isaiah to Malachi.* Copenhagen: Rosenkilde Og Bagger, 1966.

Hanson, Paul D. *The Dawn of Apocalyptic.* Philadelphia: Fortress Press, 1977.

_____. "Israelite Religion in the Early Post-Exilic Period." In *Ancient Israelite Religion: Essays in Honor of Frank Moore Cross.* Ed. Patrick D. Miller, et al. Philadelphia: Fortress Press, 1987.

_____. *The People Called.* New York: Harper and Row,1986.

Haran, Menahem. *Temples and Temple Services in Ancient Israel: An Inquiry into the Character of Cult Phenomena and the Historical Setting of the Priestly School.* Oxford: The Clarendon Press, 1978.

Harris, Marvin. *Cultural Materialism: The Struggle for a Science of Cultur.* New York: Random House, 1979.

Hayes, John H., and J. Maxwell Miller, eds. *Israelite and Judean History.* Old Testament Library. Philadelphia: Westminster Press, 1977.

Horsley, Richard A. "Empire, Temple and Community--But Not Bourgeoise!: A Response to Blenkinsopp and Peterson." In *Second Temple Studies: 1. Persian Period.* Ed. Philip R. Davies. Sheffield: Sheffield Academic Press, 1991.

Hubert, Henri, and Marcel Mauss. *Sacrifice: Its Nature and Function.* Chicago: University of Chicago Press, 1964.

Hunger, H. *Babylonische und Assyriche Kolophone.* Alter Orient und Altes Testament, vol.2. Neukirchen Vluyn: Nukirchener Verlag, 1968.

Janssen, Enno. *Judah in der Exilszeit: Ein Beitrag zur Frage der Entstehung des Judentum.* Göttingen: Vanderhoeck & Ruprecht, 1956.

Japhet, Sara. *The Ideology of the Book of Chronicles and Its Place in Biblical Thought.* Frankfurt: Verlag Peter Lang, 1989.

_____. "People and Land in the Restoration Period." In *Das Land*

Israel in Biblischer Zeit. Ed. George Strecker. Göttingen: Vandenhoeck & Ruprecht, 1981.

Kapelrud, Arvid S. *Israel from the Earliest Times to the Birth of Christ.* London: Basil Blackwell, 1966.Kaufman, Yehezkel. *From the Babylonian Captivity to the End of Prophecy.* Vol. 4 of *History of the Religion of Israel.* New York: Ktav Publishing House, 1977.

Kellerman, Ulrich. *Nehemiah: Quellen, Überlieferung, und Geschichte.* Berlin: Verlag Alfred Töpelmann, 1967.

Klein, Ralph W. *Israel in Exile: A Theological Interpretation.* Philadelphia: Fortress Press, 1979.

_____. "Ezra and Nehemiah in Recent Studies." In *Magnalia Dei: The Mighty Acts of God.* Ed. Frank Moore Cross et al. Garden City, N.J.: Doubleday & Co., 1976.

Kreissig, Heinz. *Die Sozialökonomische Situation in Juda zur Achämenidenzeit.* Berlin: Akademie-Verlag, 1973.

Leach, Edmund. "The Logic of Sacrifice." In *Anthropological Approaches to the Old Testament.* Ed. Bernhard Lang. Philadelphia: Fortress Press, 1985.

Lemche, Niels Peter. *Early Israel: Anthropological and Historical Studies on the Israelite Society before the Monarchy.* Leiden: E. J. Brill, 1985.

Levi-Strauss, Claude. *The Savage Mind.* Chicago: University of Chicago Press, 1966.

_____. *Stuctural Anthropology.* Trans. Claire Jacobson and Brooke Grundfest Schoepf. New York: Basic Books, Inc., 1963.

Lienhardt, Godfrey. *Divinity and Experience: The Religion of the Dinka.* Oxford: The Clarendon Press, 1961.

Lowery, R. H. *The Reforming Kings: Cult and Society in First Temple Judah.* Sheffield: JSOT Press, 1991.

Mack, Burton. "Introduction--Religion and Ritual." In *Violent Origins: Ritual Killing and Cultural Formation.* Ed. Robert G. Hamerton-Kelly. Stanford, Californaia: Stanford University Press, 1987.

Maier, Johann. *The Temple Scroll: An Introduction, Translation, &*

Commentary. Sheffield, England: JSOT Press, 1985.

Mallau, Hans H. "The Redaction of Ezra 4-6: A Plea for a Theology of the Scribes." In *Perspectives of the Hebrew Bible: Essays in Honor of Walter J. Harrelson*. Ed. James L. Crenshaw. Macon, Georgia: Mercer Press, 1988.

Mason, Rex. *Preaching the Tradition: Homily and Hermeneutics after the Exile*. Cambridge: Cambridge University Press, 1990.

McConville, J. G. *Law and Theology in Deuteronomy*. Sheffield: JSOT Press, 1984.

McKenzie, Steven L. *The Chronicler's Use of the Deuteronomic History*. Atlanta: Scholars Press, 1984.

Meyers, Carol L., and Eric M. *Haggai, Zechariah 1-8*. Anchor Bible. Garden City, New York: Doubleday & Co., 1987.

Meyers, Eric M. "The Persian Period and the Judean Restoration from Zerubbabel to Nehemiah." In *Ancient Israelite Religion: Essays in Honor of Frank Moore Cross*. Ed. Patrick D. Miller, et. al. Philadelphia: Fortress Press, 1987.

Milgrom, Jacob. "Hezekiah's Sacrifices at the Dedication Services of the Purified Temple." In *Biblical and Related Studies Presented to Samuel Iwry*. Ed. Ann Kort and Scott Morschauser. Winona Lake, Indiana: Eisenbrauns, 1985.

_____. "The Priestly Laws of Sancta Contamination." In *Sha'arei Talmon*. Ed. Michael Fishbane and Emanuel Tov. Winona Lake, Indiana: Eisenbrauns, 1992.

_____. *Leviticus 1-16*. Anchor Bible, vol.3. New York: Doubleday & Co., 1991.

_____. *Studies in Cultic Theology and Terminology*. Leiden: Brill, 1983.

Morgan, Donn F. *Between Text and Community: The "Writings" in Canonical Interpretation*. Minneapolis: Fortress Press, 1990.

Mosis, Rudolf. *Unterschungen zur Theologie des chronisten Geschichtesweke*. Freiberg: Herder, 1973.

Myers, Jacob M. *Ezra-Nehemiah*. Anchor Bible. Garden City, New York:

Doubleday & Co., 1966.

_____. *I and II Esdras*. Anchor Bible. Garden City, New York: Doubleday & Co., 1974.

_____. *II Chronicles*. Anchor Bible. Garden City, New York: Doubleday & Co., 1965.

Newsome, James D. ed. *A Synoptic Harmony of Samuel, Kings, and Chronicles: With Related Passages from Psalms, Isaiah, Jeremiah, and Ezra*. Grand Rapids, Michigan: Baker, 1986.

_____. *By the Waters of Babylon: An Introduction to the History and Theology of the Exile*. Atlanta: John KnoxPress, 1979.

North, Robert. "Does Archaeology Prove Chronicle's Sources?" In *A Light unto My Path: Old Testament Studies in Honor of Jacob M. Myers*. Ed. Howard N. Bream, et al. Philadelphia: Temple University Press, 1974.

Oded, Bustenay. "Judah and the Exile." In *Israelite and Judean History*. Old Testament Library. Ed. John H. Hayes and J. Maxwell Miller. Philadelphia: Westminster Press, 1977.

Oesterley, W. O. E. *Sacrifices in Ancient Israel: Their Origin, Purposes, and Development*. New York: The McMillan Company, 1937.

Petersen, David L. *Haggai and Zechariah 1-8*. Old Testament Library. Philadelphia Westminster Press, 1984.

_____. *Late Israelite Prophecy: Studies in Deutero-Prophetic Literature and Chronicles*. Missoula, Montana: Scholar's Press, 1977.

Pohlman, K. F. *Studien zum Dritten Esra*. Göttingen: Vandenhoeck und Ruprecht, 1970.

Porter, J. R. "Old Testament Historiography." In *Tradition and Interpretation*. Ed. G. W. Anderson. Oxford: Oxford University Press, 1979.

von Rad, Gerhard. *Das Geschichtsbild des Chronistischen Werkes*. Stuttgart: Kohlhammer, 1930.

_____. *Old Testament Theology*, vol. 2. Trans. D. G.M. Stalker. New York: Harper & Row, 1965.

Rogerson, John W. "Anthropology and the Old Testament." In *The World of Ancient Israel: Social, Anthropological, and Political Perspectives*. Ed. Ronald E. Clements. Cambridge: Cambridge University Press, 1989.

_____. "Sacrifice in the Old Testament: Problems of Method and Approach." In *Sacrifice*. Ed. M. E. C. Bourdillon and Meyer Fortes. New York: Academic Press, 1980.

Rothstein, J. W. *Juden und Samaritaner: Die Grundlegende Scheidung von Judentum und Heidentum*. Leipzig: J. C. Heinrichs, 1908.

Rowley, H. H. "The Chronological Order of Ezra and Nehemiah." In *Ignace Goldziher Memorial Volume*, vol. 1. Ed. D. S. Lowinger and J. Somogyi. Budapest: Globus, 1948.

Rudolph, Wilhelm. *Chronikbüchen*. Tübingen: Verlag J. C. B. Mohr, 1955.

_____. *Esra und Nehemiah*. Tübingen: Verlag J. C. B. Mohr, 1949.

Schmidt, Werner H. *The Faith of the Old Testament*. Philadelphia: Westminster Press, 1983.

Schultz, Carl. "The Political Tensions Reflected in Ezra-Nehemiah." In *Scripture in Context: Essays on the Comparative Method*. Ed. Carl D. Evans, et al. Pittsburgh: The Pickwick Press, 1980.

Schwager, Raymond. *Must There Be Scapegoats: Violence and Redemption in the Bible*. Trans. Maria L. Assad. New York: Harper & Row, 1987.

Shaver, Judson R. *Torah and the Chronicler's History Work: An Inquiry into the Chronicler's References to Laws, Festivals and Cultic Institutions in Relationship to Pentateuchal Legislation*. Atlanta: Scholars Press, 1989.

Smith, Daniel K. *The Religion of the Landless: The Social Context of the Babylonian Exile*. Bloomington, Indiana: Meyer Stone Publishing, 1989.

Smith, Mark S. *The Early History of God: Yahweh and the Other Deities in Ancient Israel*. San Fransisco: Harper & Row, 1990.

Smith, Morton. *Palestinian Parties and Politics that Shaped the Old*

Testament. London: SCM Press, 1987.

Smith, William Robertson. *Lectures on the Religion of the Semites: The Fundamental Institutions*. New York: Ktav Publishing, 1969.

Spencer, Herbert. *The Principles of Sociology*. 3rd ed. New York: D. Appleton and Co., 1896.

Stern, E. "The Persian Empire and the Political and SocialHistory of Palestine in the Persian Period." In *Introduction, the Persian Period*. Vol. 1 of *Cambridge History of Judaism*. Ed. W. D. Davies and Louis Finkelstein. New York: Columbia University Press, 1984.

Stuhlmueller, Carroll. *Rebuilding with Hope: A Commentary on the Books of Haggai and Zechariah*. Grand Rapids, Michigan: Wm. B. Eerdmans Publishing Co., 1988.

Talmon, Shemaryahu. "Ezra and Nehemiah." *Interpreter's Bible*, vol. 3. Ed. George Buttrick. Nashville: Abingdon, 1954.

Throntveit, Mark A. *When Kings Speak: Royal Speech and Royal Prayer in Chronicles*. Atlanta: Scholars Press, 1987.

Torrey, Charles C. *Ezra Studies*. New York: Ktav Publishing, 1970. . *The Chronicler's History of Israel: Chronicles-Ezra-Nehemiah Restored to its Original Form*. New Haven: Yale University Press, 1954.

_____. "A Revised View of I Esdras." In *Louis Ginzberg Jubilee Volume*. New York: American Academy for JewishResearch, 1945.

Turner, Victor. *The Drums of Affliction: A Study of Religious Processes among the Ndembu of Zambia*. Oxford: The Clarendon Press, 1968.

Tylor, Edward B. *Primitive Culture: Researches into the Development of Mythology, Philosophy, Religion, Language, Art, and Custom*. 2nd ed. New York: Henry Holt and Co., 1889.

DeVaux, Roland. *Ancient Israel: Its Life and Institutions*. Trans. John McHugh. New York: McGraw Hill Book Company, Inc., 1961.

_____. *Studies in Old Testament Sacrifice*. Cardiff: University of Wales Press, 1964.

Weinberg, J. "Die Agrarhältnisse inder Bürger-Tempel-Gemeinde der Achämenidzeit." In *Wirtschaft und Gesellschaft im Alten Vorderasien*.

124

Ed. J. Harmatta and G. Komoróczy. Tübingen: Verlag J. C. B. Mohr, 1976.

Welch, Adam C. *Post-Exilic Judaism.* London: William Blackwood & Sons, 1935.

_____. *The Work of the Chronicler: Its Purpose and Date.* London: Oxford University Press, 1939.

Whiston, William. *The Works of Josephus.* Peabody, Massachusetts: Hendrickson Publishing, 1985.

Widengren, George. "The Persian Period." In *Israelite and Judean History.* Ed. John H. Hayes and J. Maxwell Miller. Philadelphia: Westminster, 1977.

Willi, Thomas. *Die Chronik als Auslegung.* Göttingen: Vandenhoeck and Ruprecht, 1972.

Williams, James G. *The Bible, Violence and the Sacred: Liberation from the Myth of Sanctioned Violence.* San Francisco: HarperSanFrancisco, 1991.

Williamson, H. G. M. *Ezra-Nehemiah.* Word Biblical Commentary. Waco, Texas: Word Publishing, 1985.

_____. *1 and 2 Chronicles.* NCBC. Grand Rapids, Michigan: Wm. B. Eerdmans Publishing Co., 1982.

_____. *Israel in the Book of Chronicles.* London: Cambridge University Press, 1977.

Wolff, H. Werner. *Haggai.* Minneapolis: Augsburg Publishing, 1988.

Zunz, Leopold. *Die Gottes dienstlichen Vorträge der Juden, historische Entwickelt. Ein Beitrag zur Alterthummskunde und Biblischen Kritik, zur Literatur und Religionsgeschichte.* Berlin: A. Asher, 1832.

Periodicals

Ackroyd, Peter R. "Chronicles-Ezra-Nehemiah: The Concept of Unity." *Zeitschrift fur die Alttestamentliche Wissenschaft,* 100 (1988 Supplement), 189-201.

Allan, Nige. "The Identity of the Jerusalem Priesthood during the Exile." *The Hibbert Journal*, 23 (1982), 259-269.

Brindle, Wayne A. "The Origin and History of the Samaritans." *Grace Theological Journal*, 5 (1984), 47-75.

Braun, Roddy. "The Message of Chronicles: Rally Round the Temple." *Concordia Theological Monthly*, 42 (1971), 502-513.

Brueggemann, Walter. "At the Mercy of Babylon: A Subversive Rereading of the Empire." *Journal of Biblical Literature*, 110 (1991), 3-22.

Cody, A. "When Is the Chosen People Called a *Goy*." *Vetus Testamentum*, 14 (1964), 1-6.

Cross, Frank Moore. "A Reconstruction of the Judean Restoration." *Journal of Biblical Literature*, 94 (1975), 4-18.

_____. "The History of the Biblical Text in the Light of the Discoveries in the Judean Desert." *Harvard Theological Review* 57 (1964), 281-299.

Eskenazi, Tamara C. "The Chronicler and the Composition of I Esdras." *Catholic Biblical Quarterly*, 48 (1986), 39-61.

Fensham, F. C. "Some Theological and Religious Aspects in Ezra and Nehemiah." *Journal of Northwest Semitic Languages*, 11 (1983), 59-68.

Frost, Stanley Brice. "The Death of Josiah: A Conspiracy of Silence." *Journal of Biblical Literature*, 87 (1968), 369-382.

Freedman, David N. "The Chronicler's Purpose." *Catholic Biblical Quarterly*, 23 (1961), 436-442.

Haran, Menahem. "Explaining the Identical Lines at the End of Chronicles and the Beginning of Ezra." *Bible Review*, 2 (1986), 18-20.

Hendel, Ronald S. "Sacrifice as a Cultural System: The Ritual Symbolism of Exodus 24:3-8." *Zeitschrift fur die Alttestamentliche Wissenschaft*, 101 (1989), 366-390.

Hildebrand, D. R. "Temple Ritual: A Paradigm for Moral Holiness in Haggai ii 10-19." *Vetus Testamentum*, 39 (1989), 154-168.

Hogg, W. E. "The Founding of the Second Temple." *Princeton Theological Review*, 25 (1927), 457-461.

Hoonaker, A. van. "La succession chronologique Néhémie-Esdras." *Revue Biblique*, 32 (1923), 481-494.

_____. "La succession chronologique Néhémie-Esdras." *Revue Biblique*, 33 (1924), 33-64.

Japhet, Sara. "The Supposed Common Authorship of Chronicles and Ezra Investigated Anew." *Vetus Testamentum*, 18 (1969), 330-371.

Jones, Douglas R. "The Cessation of Sacrifice after theDestruction of the Temple in 586 B. C." *Journal of Theological Studies*, 14 (1963), 12-31.

Klein, Ralph W. "A Theology for Exiles." *Dialog*, 17 (1978), 128-134.

Leeseburg, Martin W. "Ezra and Nehemiah: A Review of the Return and Reform." *CTM*, 33 (1962), 79-90.

Lemke, Werner E. "The Synoptic Problem in the Chronicler's History." *Harvard Theological Review*, 58 (1965), 349-363.

Mantel, H. D. "The Dichotomy of Judaism during the Second Temple." *Annual of the Hebrew Union College*, 44 (1973), 57-86.

May, H. G. "'This People' and 'This Nation' in Haggai." *Vetus Testamentum*, 18 (1968), 190-197.

McConville, J. G. "Ezra-Nehemiah and the Fulfillment of Prophecy." *Vetus Testamentum*, 36 (1986), 205-224.

McEvenue, Sean E. "The Political Structure in Judah from Cyrus to Nehemiah." *Catholic Biblical Quarterly*, 43 (1981), 353-364.

McKenna, Andrew J. "Introduction." *Semeia*, 33 (1984), 1-11.

Milgrom, Jacob. "A Prolegomenon to Leviticus 17:11. *Journal of Biblical Literature*, 90 (1971), 149-156.

Moriarty, Frederick L. "The Chronicler's Account of Hezekiah's Reign." *Catholic Biblical Quarterly*, 27 (1965), 399-406.

Myers, Jacob M. "The Kerygma of the Chronicler." *Interpretation*, 20 (1966), 259-273.

Newsome, James D. "Toward a New Understanding of the Chronicler and His Purposes." *Journal of Biblical Literature,* 94 (1975), 201-220.

Nicholson, Ernest W. "The Meaning of the Expression *'m h'rts* in the Old Testament." *Journal of Semitic Studies,* 10 (1965), 59-66.

North, Robert. "The Theology of the Chronicler." *Journal of Biblical Literature,* 82 (1963), 369-381.

Petersen, David L. "Zechariah's Visions: A Theological Perspective." *Vetus Testamentum,* 34 (1984), 195-206.

_____. "Zerubbabel and the Second Temple Reconstruction." *Catholic Biblical Quarterly,* 36 (1974), 366-372.

Rabbe, Paul R. "Deliberate Ambiguity in the Psalter." *Journal of Biblical Literature,* 110 (1991), 213-227.

Rudolph, Wilhelm. "Problems of the Books of Chronicles." *Vetus Testamentum,* 4 (1954), 401-409.

Schottroff, W. "Zur Sozialsgeschichte Israels in der Perserzeit." *Verkündigung und Forschung,* 27 (1982), 46-68.

Snaith, Norman. "A Note on Ezra viii:35." *Journal of Theological Studies,* 22 (1971), 150-152.

Talmon, S. "Calendar-Reckoning in Ephraim and Judah." *Vetus Testamentum,* 8 (1958), 48-74.

Talshir, David. "A Reinvestigation of the LinguisticRelationship Between Chronicles and Ezra-Nehemiah." *Vetus Testamentum,* 38 (1988), 163-193.

Thomas D. Winton. "The Sixth Century B.C.: A Creative Epoch in the History of Israel." *Journal of Semitic Studies,* 6 (1961), 33-46.

Wahl, Thomas Peter. "Chronicles: The Rewriting of History." *The Bible Today,* 26 (1988), 197-202.

Wenham, J. W. "Large Numbers in the Old Testament." *Tyndale Bulletin,* 18 (1967), 19-53.

Williamson, H. G. M. "The Composition of Ezra i-iv." *Journal of*

128

Theological Studies, 33 (1983), 1-30.

_____. "Did the Author of Chronicles also Write the Books of Ezra and Nehemiah?" *Bible Review*, 3 (1987), 56-59.

_____. "Isaiah 63:7-64:11: Exilic Lament or Post-ExilicProtest?" *Zeitschrift fur die Alttestamentliche Wissenschaft*, 102 (1990), 40-58.

_____. "Laments at the Destroyed Temple." *Bible Review*, 6 (1990), 12-17, 44.

Wood, Forrest. "Averting Violence: Social and Personal." *Perspectives in Religious Studies*, 14 (1987), 29-37.

Yamauchi, Edwin M. "The Archaeological Background of Ezra."*Biblica Sacra*, 137. (1980), 195-211.

Unpublished Sources

Arnold, Bill T. "Bilingualism in Ezra and Daniel." Paper presented at Society of Bibilical Literature, Kansas City, Missouri. November 23, 1991. Personal notes.

Carter, Tom E. "The Province of Yehud in the Persian Period: A Textual, Artifacual, and Geographic Approach." Paper presented at Society of Biblical Literature, Kansas City, Missouri. November 25, 1991. Personal notes.

Chang, Wilson Ilsan. "The *Tendenz* of the Chronicler." Ph.D. dissertation, Hartford Theological Seminary, 1973.

Lo, Hing Choi. "The Structural Relationship in the Synoptic and non-Synoptic Passages in the Book of Chronicles." Ph. D. dissertation, Southern Baptist Theological Seminary, 1986.

Index of Authors

Index of Scripture References

DATE DUE

Printed
in USA